CARNY FOLK

CARNY FOLK

THE WORLD'S WEIRDEST SIDESHOW ACTS

Francine Hornberger

CITADEL PRESS
Kensington Publishing Corp.
www.kensingtonbooks.com

CITADEL PRESS BOOKS are published by

Kensington Publishing Corp.
850 Third Avenue
New York, NY 10022

Copyright © 2005 Francine Hornberger

All Kensington titles, imprints, and distributed lines are available at special quantity discounts for bulk purchases for sales promotions, premiums, fund-raising, educational, or institutional use. Special book excerpts or customized printings can also be created to fit specific needs. For details, write or phone the office of the Kensington special sales manager: Kensington Publishing Corp., 850 Third Avenue, New York, NY 10022, attn: Special Sales Department; phone 1-800-221-2647.

CITADEL PRESS and the Citadel logo are Reg. U.S. Pat. & TM Off.

First printing: April 2004

10 9 8 7 6 5 4

Printed in the United States of America

Library of Congress Control Number: 2004116400

ISBN 0-8065-2661-0

In loving memory of Spike,
the biggest freak I ever knew.

CONTENTS

Chapter 3: Armless and Legless Wonders 75

Chapter 4: More to Love 94

Chapter 5: Eerie and . . . Exotic? 108

Chapter 6: Human or Animal? 134

CONTENTS

ACKNOWLEDGMENTS

Many thanks must be extended to those who helped me during the making of this book. Without them, there would be no book. First and foremost, thanks to my editor, Gary Goldstein, for believing in and signing up this project, and for his invaluable editorial comments and guidance. Thank you also to Susan Higgins, copyeditor, who did a beautiful job making things flow just right. A special thanks also goes to production editor Arthur Maisel for making sure all the pieces fit perfectly in place, and for shepherding the project from a stack of papers and photos to the book you're now holding in your hands.

Outside the world of Citadel books, many made wonderful contributions, whether by helping me track down photos or by having rich resources of information available for my research. Thank you to: Alan Stullenbarger of Alan's Antiques, Earlyphotos.com, Jeff and Susan Murray, Andy Foot, Alex at museumofhoaxes.com, Mack Dennard, Elizabeth "GirlRat" at Phreeque.com, Laurie Block and the DisabilityMuseum.org, Bill Griffith, Tedd Webb, Jeanette Sitton and the Joseph Carey Merrick Tribute Website, the Ashleigh Hotel, the Library of Congress, Todd Robbins, and Jennifer Miller.

Lastly, my heartfelt gratitude goes out to my friends and family, especially to my new in-laws, for understanding why I need to "disappear" sometimes. Above all, thank you to my husband, Christopher LaSala, for putting up with me while I was in the throes of completing this project. His patience and support are simply miraculous.

INTRODUCTION

Sometime in 2003, my husband and I started watching the HBO show *Carnivale*. Exactly why we were drawn to it is pretty much a mystery. Neither of us had ever had any interest in sideshows or circuses before. However, there was just something so mesmerizing about the show—like we were watching something we really should not have been, but we couldn't—and wouldn't—look away.

Carnivale, of course, has many levels to it, but that's not why we started watching it. We wanted to see Siamese twins. We wanted to watch armless people do things with their feet—that kind of thing.

As we moved through each episode, I found myself becoming more and more curious about the characters—not just what was going to happen to the specific characters in the show; it was more a sweeping curiosity about what had inspired these characters. I wanted to immerse myself in that world and see what it was all about, so I called my editor and suggested that I write a book.

When I started telling friends and family members that I was writing this book, however, reactions ran the gamut from confused to horrified, with only a few glints of intrigue.

Why the shock? In our times, we have become so politically correct that we blindly accept and enforce the black-and-white boundaries that have been imposed upon us. We don't easily accept that there are, indeed, shades of gray. In the modern world, people typically look down on—or, more accurately, *away from*—freakaphiles. That's not surprising: it's been ingrained in the popular consciousness to be shocked and offended.

We need to get over ourselves.

Certainly I wasn't alone in my fascination. My husband and I were not the only two people in America who tuned in to gawk every week. The success of *Carnivale* comes as little surprise to anyone who understands anything about human nature and curiosity about the strange, the unusual, the freakish—from the dawn of the human race to the present day.

Human curiosities have been around as long as there have been human beings, and the general public has always been fascinated by them. Why the fascination? "Regular" folks love glimpsing and experiencing things they will never experience firsthand and which scare as much as they captivate.

This fascination really exploded into high gear in the mid-1800s. With the industrial revolution in full swing, people found themselves having plenty of something they never had before: leisure time.

One of the first, and certainly the most famous, individuals to capitalize on this was Phineas Taylor Barnum (see page 8). In 1841, he became proprietor of the American Museum in New York City. Here, he showcased contortionists, a tattooed man, and similar acts. As his notoriety grew, he built his enterprise to feature bearded ladies, albinos, giants and dwarfs, and other folks too "odd" to walk unnoticed among the general population.

By the 1870s, museums of this type began popping up all over the nation—the world—and eventually began to travel. It was these traveling oddity museums, which became linked to circuses and carnivals, that eventually became known as "sideshows."

Anyone who has done his or her homework on the history of the sideshow knows that for the most part, sideshow oddities were treated with respect. They were the bread and butter of the show, and they were, for the most part, regarded as such. It was rare that disabilities were emphasized; instead, the draw lay in the "can-do."

The late "Human Blockhead" Melvin Burkhart (see page 166), who was not a natural-born freak but a man who "freakified" himself by learning to swallow swords, contort his body, and pound spikes into his head, explained it best: "We would never get up there and just say, 'Come in here and see a horrible person.'... You wouldn't go

LIBRARY OF CONGRESS

Phineas Taylor Barnum

in there and say, 'You're going to see a girl with no arms doing everything with her feet. You're going to see the armless wonder who does fantastic things right before your eyes using nothing but the tootsies on her feet.'"

In the heyday of the sideshow, human curiosities were revered all over the world. People like Tom Thumb (see page 13) and his wife Lavinia Warren (see page 19) received wedding presents from Queen Victoria, a known freak aficionada. They weren't alone.

Todd Robbins (see page 181), a performer-impresario at the forefront of the next wave of sideshow mania, has explained: "The freaks were the royalty of the sideshow. They truly belonged and they were not victims. . . . When audiences walked away after seeing the extraordinary things people could do—like the seal-boy whose hands extended from his shoulders, writing beautifully—they said, 'What an amazing person,' not 'there but for the grace of God go I.'"

But then the pendulum swung.

Even from the very beginning, doctors and scientists have objected to "freaks" making livings as exhibits. They felt it would be better to have these specimens in the laboratory, where they could study them, perhaps "fix" them, and make new advances in teratology, the study of *monsters*. And, incidentally, the doctors and scientists hadn't intended to pay for the privilege.

Sideshow freaks never saw themselves as "monsters" who needed to be "studied for the good of humankind"—nor had their fans. Jeanie Tomaini, grand dame of freaks, said that "Every once in a while, Mother Nature makes a goof. . . . But on this show, they could earn their livings and very, very few of the sideshow people I ever heard of asked for food stamps or anything else for help. I'm very proud of the people I know that they do stand on their own two feet."

Ironically, the group that worked the hardest to snuff out the opportunity for the unusual to stand on their own two feet were human rights activists, who most sideshow folk refer to as "do-gooders"—and those quotation marks are intentional.

When I first began the research for this book, I thought to myself, what a tragedy of humanity were these sideshows; this could never go on in a more politically correct world. But the more I investigated, the more I learned. Certainly there was exploitation, but that can be said of any industry—music, publishing, you name it. However, what the sideshow did was provide opportunities for people who could not make livings in traditional ways to, in most cases, make fantastic livings. In contrast, for the most part, if these people were not making a living in the sideshow, they'd be dying slowly in institutions.

Carny Folk: The World's Weirdest Sideshow Acts pulls back the curtain on the most famous sideshow acts of all time, providing biographical information on each subject as well as explanations for "how they got that way," "how they did that," and why. Behind every successful sideshow act, there's an impresario who knew the secrets of key publicity and positioning. Throughout this book, you'll meet some of them, too.

Today, the attraction to sideshows and their promise to show the incredible, the unbelievable, and the preposterous is experiencing a renaissance. *Carnivale* is only part of it. Performers and impresarios like Todd Robbins, Jennifer Miller (see page 175), and Jim Rose (see page 204), in their own ways, are providing new bents for this entertainment venue. Plus, there's a whole new generation of "carny kids" emerging, as featured in a six-page article in *Rolling Stone* magazine in September 2003. Who knows what the future holds?

Whatever you're inclined to believe, if you are reading this, you are most likely one of us. . . . gooble gobble . . . and not to worry: Curiosity is not offensive; closed mindedness is.

Well, come on. Let's go see the freaks.

You know you want to.

Petite Performers and Tall Orders

Che Mah

a.k.a. "The World's Smallest Human"

(1838–1926)

> Have traveled most all around the world and
> have appeared before the crowned heads of
> Europe. The opinion of the press and the public
> is that I am the smallest man in the world.
>> —Che Mah, from his cartes de visites

Che Mah was a marvel in miniature. Like any of the "little people" featured in this chapter, he never let his height get in the way. In fact, aside from the fact that his diminutive stature allowed him to make a living in show business, it was never an encumbrance.

Che Mah was born on April 13, 1838, in Ningpo, a small farming village on the island of Choo-Sang, off the coast of China. His parents, both of normal size and stature, didn't believe their son could be of much help to them in cultivating their land. But as Che

Mah got older, he showed that not only was he able to help, but that he was an asset. Whether or not Che Mah had siblings is unknown.

At the time Che Mah was growing up, internationally known impresario P. T. Barnum (see page 8) was dispatching scouts around the world to search out human oddities. It took them a while to make it to China, but luckily for Barnum and for Che Mah, his agents did make it there. At that time, the early 1880s, Che Mah was pretty well adapted into his farmer's life, so agents had to hard sell Che Mah on the life of fame and luxury that would be his if he went with them. Ultimately, Che Mah could not refuse. He officially joined up with Barnum in 1881. By that time, he was already forty-three years old, which was old compared with the age most sideshow performers began their careers, some even from infancy.

Che Mah was an instant sensation. He was twenty-eight inches tall, forty pounds and, at his age, he would not grow any larger. That was good news for Barnum, who always showcased little people (midgets, before the era of political correctness) to great success—and the smaller and better proportioned they were, the better. Che Mah's popularity was enhanced by the fact that he was one of the only little people—if not *the* only—still working for Barnum. Barnum's former petite stars Tom Thumb (see page 13) and Lavinia Warren (see page 19) had all but retired; Commodore Nutt (see page 7) had just recently passed away. The public was hungry for the next big little thing, and they found it in Che Mah. And, in addition to his unbelievable size, he was Asian and exotic, which was especially appealing to Americans at the end of the nineteenth century.

Barnum treated Che Mah as he did all his beloved little people. He spent tons of money having only the most lavish and sumptuous costumes made for him. He provided him with a hefty salary and anything he wanted. Although according to speculation Barnum did not always treat the performers in his employ properly, this was never true when it came to his prized little ones, as we will see.

Eventually, Che Mah's contract with Barnum's operation ran out; Barnum died in 1891, and without him there, Che Mah decided to move on. He toured with several traveling sideshows, including Buffalo Bill Cody's Wild West Show and others. He clocked a lot of miles—and experiences—into his nearly twenty-five-year career.

In about 1905, Che Mah got bored with show business. Yes, he had had the opportunity to tour the world, appearing before and with all kinds of VIPs, including monarchs and dignitaries. But at this point, he was nearly seventy years old. He was tired—of the business, that is; otherwise he was a bundle of energy. Even though he was pushing seventy, he was ready to embark on the next phase of his life. With the money he had accumulated from his years on the road, Che Mah purchased a farm in rural Indiana, near Eagle Lake, because, of all the places he had traveled to and seen, it most reminded him of the home he had left behind. Why he didn't return to Ningpo is unknown.

Unfortunately, farming was not a successful endeavor for Che Mah. Because of his height, it took him forever and a day to harness his horses, and by the time he had exhausted himself with that task, he still had to plow his fields. Che Mah had no choice but to sell the farm and look for something else to do. He moved to the less rural Knox, Indiana, but not before getting married, for the first time, at seventy years old!

When Che Mah bought his farm, he hired a woman to help out around the house while he worked the fields. The woman, Nora Cleveland, was reportedly 5 feet, 8 inches tall (that's 68 inches, or 40 inches—3¼ feet—taller than Che Mah) and weighed more than 200 pounds. This, remarkably, is the woman who became his wife.

Fifteen years into the marriage, Che Mah filed for divorce. Apparently, his wife had stopped giving the randy eighty-five-year-old dwarf enough sex, and he divorced his wife on those grounds. Three years later, on March 21, 1926, Che Mah died. He was eighty-eight years old.

Che Mah is buried in Knox, in Crown Hill Cemetery, under a polished-granite headstone about four feet high.

The Schneider Family

a.k.a. "The Earles Family"
a.k.a. "The Doll Family"

Kurt "Harry" Earles (1902–1985)
Freida "Grace" Earles (c. 1904–1970)
Hilda "Daisy" Earles (1907–1980)
Elly "Tiny" Earles (c. 1910–?)

> A dwarf standing on the shoulders of a giant may
> see farther than the giant himself.
>
> —Seventeenth-century poet Robert Burton

It is a rarity that into any given family, a child will be born a dwarf or midget. That two will be born is a marvel; more than two is a miracle—or a curse, depending on your perspective. In the case of the Schneider family of Stolpen, Germany, four children out of seven were midgets; for them, it proved to be a miracle. It goes without saying that Emma and Gustav Schneider were initially confused that several of their children born in sequence were smaller than average, but in time, they were able to see the advantage.

Unfortunately, exact dates of birth are not available for all the Schneider children. Facts, especially when it comes to sideshow performers, notoriously get lost to time. At least two birthdates can be confirmed; the others have been estimated based on when the children became old enough to leave Germany to work in the United States. Kurt, the oldest of the quartet, was born on April 3, 1902. Freida followed, but her exact date of birth isn't known. She was the second child in birth order, so she had to have been born some time between 1903 and 1906. Hilda was born on April 29, 1907. There's also no exact date of birth for the youngest, Elly, though it is estimated that she was born sometime around 1910.

It took until well after Elly was born for Emma and Gustav to realize that they weren't being punished by God, but instead were sitting on a potential gold mine. To that end, they made sure that each of their small wonders took singing and dancing lessons.

The Schneider Family

Soon, the tiny Schneiders began touring throughout Europe with their parents and other siblings. They performed in Paris, London, and all the major cities. Although they were making a good living at it, they realized that to really make the big time, they had to go to the United States. This was where little people like Tom Thumb (see page 13) and Lavinia Warren (see page 19) became legends. In the States, there would always be work. In 1915, the two oldest, Kurt and Freida, packed their bags and boarded a ship to America in the custody of the Schneider family's manager, Bert W. Earles. It wasn't long before they became a hit.

Their first booking was with the Buffalo Bill Show. They performed as "The World's Smallest Dancing Couple," and they toured under the names Hans and Gretl. This wasn't the only time they'd change their names. Soon, they Americanized their names to Harry and Grace and took on their manager's last name, Earles, as their own.

In 1922, Hilda joined her successful siblings in the States. As soon as she touched down on American soil, she shrugged her Hilda handle in favor of the ultra-American "Daisy" and also took on the Earles surname. Finally, in 1926, young Elly reunited with the group and they again became a full-fledged family act.

From the early 1920s and for the next thirty years, the family toured with Ringling Bros. and Barnum & Bailey Circus. In the tradition of glam-midgets of the past, the family spent their time dolled up in sparkling costumes, parading around on miniature ponies and existing for the pure enjoyment of the beholder. However, the family also incorporated their song-and-dance training into their act and became an even bigger hit. When Bert Earles died in the early 1930s, they decided to change the name of their act to "The Doll Family." This wasn't much of a stretch; it's what they had been nicknamed by adoring audiences who thought they looked just like a family of living dolls.

The advent of the motion picture was timed perfectly with the Doll siblings' rise to stardom. All the members of the Doll Family appeared on the big screen at one point or another, though Harry secured most of the movie work. In 1925, he played a ruthless midget named Tweedledee in the classic silent Lon Chaney Sr. hit *The Unholy Three*. A young director named Tod Browning had cast Harry in the film, and their working relationship was not forgotten when it came time for Browning to begin casting for a later project in which Harry would clinch a leading role. Other films costarring Harry included *That's My Baby* (1926), *Baby Clothes* (1926), *Baby Brother* (1927), *Special Delivery* (1927)—with Laurel and Hardy— and *Sailors Beware* (1927).

The biggest break in film came in the early 1930s, when two of the family members would play leads. (They weren't billed as leads, of course.) In *Freaks* (1932), Harry and Daisy played Hans and Freida, respectively. In the film, they are affianced and happy until Hans becomes enamored with "big person" trapeze queen Cleo. Cleo ends up marrying Hans for his money and tries to poison him on their wedding night, all in front of the devoted doe-eyed Freida.

Filled as it was with an assortment of human oddities (many of whom you'll meet later in this book), the world was unprepared for the impact Browning's *Freaks* would have on audiences everywhere. Not since 1931's *Frankenstein* had a movie so horrified moviegoers. Metro-Goldwyn-Mayer yanked *Freaks* from circulation. It was banned in Britain for more than thirty years and rarely seen in the United States until the 1960s. More than seventy years later, it still packs a wallop.

In 1939, all four Dolls acted in the Academy Award–winning Technicolor treat *The Wizard of Oz*. The girls played chorus munchkins; Harry was the mayor of the Lollipop Guild.

As much as they liked making films, however, the circus was their bread and butter. They always found themselves very comfortable with circus work, so when their stint with Ringling Bros. ended, they moved on to work with the Christiani Circus.

In 1958, the family decided, as a group, that it was time to retire, so they quit show business and bought a house together in Sarasota, Florida, where they all lived out their remaining days.

Grace was the first to pass away. She died on March 16, 1970. Ten years later, nearly to the day, on March 15, 1980, Daisy passed on. In May 1985, Harry died. At the time of this writing, in 2004, no documentation of Tiny's death can be found; according to the Internet Movie Database, she was still alive as of March 2001.

George Washington Morrison Nutt
a.k.a. "Commodore Nutt"
(1844–1881)

> [Commodore Nutt] is altogether the nicest
> little chap of his age.
> —from an article in *Scientific American*,
> February 21, 1863

Most commonly known as the "jilted" suitor of Lavinia Warren (see page 19), George Washington Morrison Nutt was a formidable celebrity in and of himself. The "rivalry"—exaggerated as it may have been—that existed between Tom Thumb (see page 13) and

---

LEGENDARY IMPRESARIO

PHINEAS TAYLOR BARNUM
(1810–1891)

In the realm of the showman, there is no one anywhere near as impressive as was Phineas Taylor Barnum. He not only invented the distinction of impresario, he mastered the enterprise of publicity and marketing and turned it into an art form. Barnum had a tendency from time to time to exaggerate—and even lie—about attractions to make them more irresistible to his public, and, fraud or not, the public ate it up. He was both detested and revered because of it, and he will forever be known as the king of all humbugs.

P. T. was born in 1810 in Bethel, Connecticut. His father, Phino, died when Barnum was only sixteen years old, and he set out to support himself and take the burden off his mother, Irena Taylor. He worked as a store clerk in Brooklyn, New York, and dreamed of making the big time.

In 1835, Barnum created the first of many international sensations. He toured an old woman, Joice Heth, who he claimed was 161 years old and the former nurse of President George Washington. After she died, an autopsy revealed she was probably closer to 75 or 80. Not a problem for Barnum. He unapologetically (which was part of the game) moved on to the next attraction, a Swedish songstress.

Nutt certainly did a little something to fuel the sparks of his own fame, but Nutt did all right on his own. He lived the life of an amicable bachelor. He was smart, he was shrewd, and he was all class.

Born in Manchester, New Hampshire, on April 1, 1844, Nutt could very well have been seen as his family's little April Fool's joke, but that wouldn't last. When Nutt was still quite young, Barnum discovered him, and if anyone had not taken Nutt seriously before this point, well, the joke would soon be on them.

Unlike his other draws, Jenny Lind was not a human oddity or freak; she was a normal girl who happened to have a pleasant singing voice. Barnum played her up as if she were the most talented person who ever lived and essentially made her a sensation, the Britney Spears of her day—albeit less naked.

Barnum built the American Museum in New York City in 1842 as a venue to show off his oddities and attractions. His all-time biggest attraction came in 1842, when he transformed toddler Charles Stratton into General Tom Thumb (see page 13). It is reported that more than 20 million paid to see Mr. Thumb. Barnum also made a fortune touring with his acts all over the United States, Europe, and even Asia and Australia.

To list the acts Barnum exhibited at his museum would be to regurgitate half this book here. Suffice to say, Barnum had much success with his venture, and he even retired from the business in the mid-1850s. Soon, a bad investment brought him back.

Unfortunately for Barnum, he lost not one but two of his dime museums to fire in the 1860s. He was in such dire straits after the second that his good friend, Tom Thumb, came out of retirement to bail Barnum out.

In the 1870s, Barnum renamed his venture "The Greatest Show on Earth." In 1881, he teamed up with a partner, James Bailey, and their collaboration became a traveling circus that exhibited human oddities "on the side," bringing into the language the term "sideshow."

Barnum passed away on April 7, 1891.

In the early 1860s, Barnum begged the wee George Washington Nutt to join him in New York, but Nutt played it coy with the seasoned showman. He made Barnum believe that he could not—"would" not—comprehend that being an exhibit in a museum was in his best interest, though, knowing all about the success of Tom Thumb, he knew differently. Nutt was a smart businessman and he felt that if he held out long enough, he would be aptly rewarded. He was right.

Nutt is at the far left, standing next to Lavinia Warren.

LIBRARY OF CONGRESS

Barnum not only promised to make Nutt a star, but assured him that if he left New England for New York, Nutt would become wealthy beyond his wildest dreams, and maybe even find true love. Though the prospect of romance may have sweetened the deal for Nutt, money was what made up his mind. In 1862, Barnum paid Nutt $30,000 to come on board. Some sources say that after this bonus, Nutt was to be paid a sum of $8,000 for a three-year contract with Barnum. No one before had ever been offered such an extraordinarily huge sum to join on with Barnum, and no one after. Besides his salary, Nutt would also be entitled to keep all the money he made selling his *cartes de visites*, the cards various acts handed out to the public with their picture on the front and sometimes a mini-bio or signature on the back.

As he was apt to do, Barnum bought elaborate and wickedly expensive costumes for his brand new mini-star. He also wrote Nutt's routines for him. He bestowed upon Nutt the title of "Commodore" and fabricated a hero's past for him, though Nutt, at eighteen years of age, was barely old enough for military service, let alone having risen to such a remarkable post.

Like Thumb, Nutt's act consisted of parading himself about in his official uniform, cracking jokes, and discussing with his audience all his many adventures. He was a hit, because of his performance and because of his size. Commodore Nutt was even tinier than Tom Thumb. Fully grown, he stood forty-three inches and weighed less than seventy pounds.

A similar act wasn't going to be the only thing Nutt shared with Tom Thumb. From the time Nutt first laid eyes on Lavinia Warren (see page 19), he was smitten. He was determined to win her and made a valiant play for her affections. Sadly for him, Lavinia's heart, as it turned out, would belong to his rival.

Nutt was nothing if not a gentleman, and when Thumb won Lavinia's heart and her hand, Nutt reacted with grace and dignity. Initially, Barnum asked Nutt to be the best man at the wedding. Nutt politely refused, explaining that this offer needed to come from the right person. When the situation was handled properly, and Thumb asked Nutt to stand up for him, Nutt graciously accepted the honor.

As much as the press, and Barnum, seemed determined to play up Nutt's broken heart, describing him as wearing "a pink under vest, *typifying easy hopes*, as the blue of the groom spoke of secured happiness," he was perfectly composed throughout the nuptials. And, as a gesture of goodwill, or so it was intended, he presented the bride with "an elegant diamond ring" as a wedding gift.

Nutt may not have gotten the girl, but this meant he never had to share anything he had with anyone else. And he had plenty: property, horses, houses—and money.

From 1869 to 1872, Nutt toured throughout Europe with General and Mrs. Thumb, and Lavinia's sister, Minnie Warren. Although sparks were rumored to have flown between Nutt and Minnie, they were never romantically involved, let alone married, which many people of the time suspected as they traveled throughout Europe with the Strattons.

Lavinia herself confirmed this in her autobiography (published in 1906 in installments in the *New York Tribune Sunday Magazine*). "Here I will refute a general impression which meets me everywhere I go: which is that Minnie married Commodore Nutt. This impression arose . . . from the fact that the Commodore was groomsman at the marriage of General Tom Thumb and myself, and my sister officiated as bridesmaid. Then they were with us in our subsequent travels . . . and completed our quartet around the world." Minnie, herself, did marry a "little man," but it was not Commodore Nutt, it was Major Edward Newell.

After this tour, Nutt was fatigued. His obligation to Barnum well past fulfilled, he decided to retire. Nutt had a brother, Rodney, who was also a little person, and who had established a life for himself in San Francisco. Nutt moved to San Francisco to be with Rodney for his remaining days.

In 1881, Nutt came down with a kidney condition called Bright's disease. This condition can be treated today, but no treatment or remedy for it existed in the late nineteenth century: It was a death sentence. George Washington Morrison Nutt died on a visit to New York on March 25, 1881.

Charles Sherwood Stratton

a.k.a. "Tom Thumb"
a.k.a. "General Tom Thumb"
(1838–1883)

> The charming man in miniature is undoubtedly
> by far the smallest man alive, of his age. He is
> intelligent, sprightly, educated, perfectly
> symmetrical in all his proportions, and graceful
> beyond belief.
>
> —From an 1860 advertisement of the
> General Tom Thumb attraction

Although there were human oddities exhibited before Tom Thumb, he will forever be known as the first to ever become an international sensation. And, besides being Barnum's most famous act ever, he was also the showman's closest friend. Barnum "saved" Tom when he was a young child and gave him a chance to be someone successful; later in his life, Thumb returned the favor.

On January 4, 1838, Bridgeport, Connecticut, welcomed its most famous resident. Charles Sherwood Stratton was born to parents Sherwood Edwards Stratton, a carpenter, and Cynthia Stratton, née Thompson, an inn worker. They had no idea what the future held.

By all accounts, young Charles was normal. The third of four children, he came into the world a full-sized infant, weighing more than nine pounds. For months after his birth, he continued to grow, but then mysteriously he stopped at six months old. He was just shy of two feet tall and fifteen pounds—just six pounds more than his birth weight—and remained that size well into his teens. Eventually, he shot up to three feet, four inches, but that would be much later. (At the time of his death, he had grown to forty inches and weighed seventy-five pounds.)

Reportedly, Charles's parents were quite ashamed of their third-born, and generally kept him hidden away. They had no idea why this terrible tragedy had befallen them, and guessed that "maternal impression" was probably the culprit. (In the nineteenth century,

Charles Sherwood Stratton

and well before, people believed that birth defects were caused by a phenomenon called *maternal impression*. In short, if the pregnant mother saw something distressing, the baby would be born echoing what she had seen.) When Cynthia was pregnant with Charles, the family puppy had drowned before her own eyes and she was not able to save him. The puppy would never "grow" to adulthood; therefore, Charles would spend his life "puppy sized."

Charles would have probably remained the family embarrassment—not to mention the constant reminder of the death of the beloved pet—had impresario P. T. Barnum not discovered him. In the autumn of 1842, Barnum happened to be in Bridgeport on business. Local word about the small Stratton boy piqued his curiosity. Barnum headed to the Stratton home for a glimpse of the boy. It proved to be a most fortuitous meeting for little Charles—and for Barnum—and the courses of many lives were immediately changed.

Barnum saw the potential in the small boy and knew he could make him into a national treasure. He *had* to exhibit the boy at his new American Museum in New York City. He made the Strattons a very generous offer, and soon was headed back to New York with his extraordinary new discovery in tow. Charles was just four years old.

As soon as they arrived in New York, Barnum went to work making his little person a must-see sensation. First, he changed the child's age from four to eleven, possibly to quell objections that Barnum would be putting such a young child to work. Next, he changed Stratton's name. For maximum impact, Barnum chose a name that might be at least vaguely familiar to his audience and also create an instant connection. He named the tot "Tom Thumb," after the dwarf knight in King Arthur's court. As the icing on the cake, Barnum added the distinction of "General" to Tom's name and changed his place of birth from Bridgeport to London. The latter wasn't much of a stretch as Stratton himself was of English ancestry; the former was just ridiculous but the public embraced it all the same.

Barnum had an exquisite wardrobe custom made for Thumb that was also extremely expensive. No matter for Barnum. He knew the more he put into the Thumb persona, the more he'd receive from it.

If everything worked out to plan, Barnum would make his invest-ment back in a snap. And he did.

With the tagline of "The Perfect Man in Miniature," General Tom Thumb made his first appearance at the Barnum Museum on Decem-ber 8, 1842. According to Barnum's well-constructed hype, General Thumb was going to be wearing an outfit "of the most splendid and superb description," and deliver a performance that promised to be "elegant, unique, amusing, and enchanting." It worked. More than 30,000 people lined up to see Thumb in the first week.

Initially like most of Barnum's performers, Thumb's act was to stand around and let people gawk at him, which was okay because the young child was painfully shy. Once he built up his courage, however, Thumb began hamming it up. Barnum taught him to per-form skits and sing and dance. Soon, Thumb was doing imperson-ations of famous little people, from Cupid to Napoleon. The shy kid became a true showman.

When the initial novelty of Thumb had worn off in New York, Barnum toured Tom around the country; Thumb proved to be as big a hit elsewhere as he was in New York. In 1844, Barnum and Thumb headed across the pond and toured Europe for three years. Ameri-cans were so distressed to see their tiny treasure leave that more than 10,000 people showed up at the harbor to wish him bon voyage.

Overseas, Thumb became the darling of European royalty, including Prince Albert and Queen Victoria. (Queen Victoria was a big fan of human curiosities and befriended many of them; Tom was always a personal favorite.) The king and queen just adored Tom and showered him with expensive gifts, including a coach the queen had specially made for him. The coach was three feet tall, four feet long, and it was designed to be pulled by a team of miniature horses. Thumb also met with Queen Isabella of Spain, King Louis Philippe of France, and other dignitaries and royals—all received him with open arms.

Back in the States, the fervor Thumb had ignited and left behind was still blazing. No one forgot about him while he was away; it was rather the opposite. Americans followed Thumb's travels through newspaper accounts fueled by publicity genius Barnum. The people were anxious to have him back.

Wherever Tom Thumb traveled, women were compelled to kiss him. Reportedly, General Tom Thumb had been kissed by more than 1 million in his life. In an 1847 article in *Littell's Living Age*, Thumb talked openly and candidly about the attention. He said, "The kissing of . . . my own countrywomen, was terrible cautious; nothing more than what you might call respect with the chill off. . . . As if they thought they was [*sic*] doing me a service, and not themselves an honor." Apparently, Europe was different: "English kissing is mighty pleasant. . . . in Scotland I was only kissed at private parties. . . . In public, the ladies used to blow kisses with their fingers." French women "so often left the paint upon my nose."

In the late 1840s, Thumb agreed to a full examination by a team of doctors, who also couldn't wait to get their hands on him. They reported that "the head of General Tom Thumb has been examined . . . the size of the brain is the smallest recorded of one capable of sane and somewhat vigorous mental manifestation." Also, "his intellectual acquirements are said to be very limited as yet." In all fairness, Thumb was only about ten years old at this time, though the world believed him to be more like seventeen. Doctors also reported that Thumb's "muscular system has attained a degree of firmness, strength, and maturity, quite equal to, or rather beyond, the average of his age." Which, again, considering his true age, was quite remarkable; at age ten, Thumb was considered to be stronger and in better physical shape than most seventeen-year-olds.

For the next decade, Thumb's popularity never diminished. Despite all the new acts Barnum brought to his American Museum, the wee general remained the top attraction. And Thumb made more money than he knew what to do with. He invested in real estate and owned several homes. He had horses. He had servants. But something was definitely missing.

Over the years, Barnum had tried to introduce Thumb to various little women, but when Tom Thumb met Lavinia Warren (see page 19), Barnum's most prized miniature woman, Thumb was hooked. There was a glitch, however. Barnum had already made up his mind that he was going to set up Lavinia with one of his other famed little people, Commodore Nutt (see page 7). Tom was not about to give up. There was a rivalry between the two men over Lavinia. Nutt was reportedly utterly smitten with her, but it is likely that this infatuation was inflated for publicity purposes.

Eventually, Tom won Lavinia over, and a whirlwind courtship ended in the wedding of the century, in 1862, which will be detailed more in Lavinia's own profile (see page 19). In short, there were 2,000 guests, all of which were the most distinguished people of the day. The couple received incredibly lavish gifts from every wealthy and famous person imaginable—and right smack in the middle of the Civil War.

After the wedding, the miniature marrieds embarked on a world tour of the United States and Europe. In total, they visited 587 cities and made an incredible 1,471 appearances over the course of three years.

When Tom Thumb and Lavinia met, Tom had stopped exhibiting. He had officially retired at the age of twenty, wealthy beyond his wildest dreams. To help his good friend Barnum out, however, he still made sporadic appearances with Barnum's show. Most significantly, it was Thumb who saved Barnum from debtor's prison and starvation when not one, but two of his dime museums burned to the ground.

In 1881, Lavinia and Tom were staying in a hotel which caught fire; the Thumbs escaped just in time. Lavinia believed that her husband never quite recovered from the experience, and she was probably right. Now in his forties, Thumb was old beyond his years. A lifetime of travel and excess made him feel more like seventy. But despite his ill health, Tom was still making appearances up until his death.

Tom Thumb died from a stroke on July 15, 1883. It is said that Barnum never got over his little friend's death. The entire country was also devastated to have lost their tiny treasure. An astonishing 10,000 mourners attended his funeral. Thumb was buried in his hometown of Bridgeport.

Surprisingly, Tom Thumb left nothing behind. Somehow, at the time of his death, all the money he and Lavinia had managed to accumulate was gone.

Lavinia Warren

a.k.a. "Mrs. Tom Thumb"
a.k.a. "The Little Queen of Beauty"
a.k.a. "The Smallest Woman Alive"
a.k.a. "The Countess Magri"
(1841–1919)

> We saw a miniature woman—aye, and the queen
> of them. Her face is bright and sweet, her eyes
> brilliant and intelligent, her form faultless, and her
> manner that of the woman of the world. What more
> could we desire?
>
> —A description of Lavinia Warren,
> the *New York Times*, December 23, 1862

The above write-up of Lavinia Warren illustrates just how people felt about her in her lifetime. Lavinia was a goddess among little people and regular-sized women alike. So loved and adored was she, in fact, that the public never really got tired of her, which is unusual for someone so famous who lived as long as she did.

Mercy Lavinia Warren Bump was born on October 31, 1841, in Middleboro, Massachusetts. Some sources report her birth year as 1842; however, in her own autobiography, Lavinia declared 1841. Ironically, Lavinia's father, James S. Bump, stood six feet tall, at a time when six feet was considered an impressive, above-average height. No firm documentation exists of Lavinia's mother's exact size, but Huldah P. Bump, had, herself, been considered "a large woman."

Lavinia grew up in a large New England family, with four brothers and three sisters. All the other children in Lavinia's family were of normal size except for one. Huldah "Minnie" Warren, born June 8, 1846 (died 1878 during childbirth), was even tinier than Lavinia. Minnie was the closest member of the family to Lavinia and would later tour extensively with her older sister.

Lavinia, the future phenom, was perfectly normal until she was

LIBRARY OF CONGRESS

Lavinia Warren

about a year old when she, in her own words, "grew in five years what an ordinary child would grow in one." She was born at a respectable six pounds, but after the first year of her life, she stopped growing considerably. For the next nine years, she managed to grow to thirty-two inches and twenty-nine pounds, and then she stopped growing completely. Yet, despite her diminutive stature, she was perfectly formed in every way; the tiny parts of her body all flowed together in a symmetrical harmony. In addition, she was exceedingly beautiful, highly intelligent, and extremely refined.

She was also something of a scamp. Lavinia never had any issue with her size; rather, she liked to use it to playfully torment others. Reportedly, Lavinia was something of a prankster in school. She would set people up and then hide where no one else could fit so she wouldn't get caught.

When she was about fifteen years old, Lavinia became a teacher, and this time, she played pranks on her students. All of her students were, naturally, taller than she was, but she quickly earned their respect by letting them know that even though she was small, they would have a pretty tough time pushing her around.

At sixteen, Lavinia found an unexpected opportunity to make a career change. A cousin, known only as Colonel Wood, came to visit the Warrens, no doubt having heard about his extraordinary cousin. History documents that the cousin operated a "floating palace of curiosities," which sailed down the Ohio and Mississippi rivers. Upon meeting Lavinia, he was absolutely entranced, and he pleaded with her parents to allow Lavinia to work with him. They ultimately conceded and Lavinia agreed.

It was an early taste of what was to come for Lavinia. She was an instant sensation and enjoyed her experience as a walking exhibit. She also made the acquaintance of many famous people, who were instantly charmed by her, including Ulysses S. Grant. The more people heard about the delightful tiny beauty, the more they were compelled to come meet her for themselves. Soon, Lavinia was regularly being called upon by the most upper-crust members of high society; even the Vanderbilts and the Astors traveled to meet her.

In 1861, P. T. Barnum learned of the existence of an exquisite miniature woman. He tracked down Lavinia and went aggressively after her. Lavinia was intrigued, but her parents were a bit unsure about Barnum and what he wanted from their daughter and how he would treat her. They believed him to be a shameless exploiter of freaks and a sketchy businessman at best. Barnum, being Barnum, was eventually able to win them over. Of course, a large up-front cash advance didn't hurt.

Once in his employ, Barnum transformed Lavinia into a mini-mega-goddess. In his autobiography, he wrote, "I purchased a very splendid wardrobe for Miss Warren, including scores of the richest dresses that could be procured, costly jewels, and in fact everything that could add to the charms of her naturally charming little person." He was very serious about her. He knew from his experience with Tom Thumb (see page 13) what riches could be made in the proper care and handling of a little person. He was thrilled to now have a little woman to dress and show and was convinced he could be even more successful with Lavinia than he had been with Tom.

Barnum eventually offered Lavinia $1,000 a week to exhibit herself at his museum. His starting offer was not as grand, but she was a very shrewd businesswoman and she held out on him. She knew he needed her more than she needed him and she drove a hard bargain. And she continued to play with him; Lavinia had already made arrangements to travel to Europe, and she told him she was going to have to finish her tour before she signed on with him. Barnum had no choice but to give in to her, which was fine. He knew his patience with Lavinia would eventually pay off.

When she returned from Europe, Lavinia was a smash in Barnum's museum. Thumb had already retired and, even though Commodore Nutt (see page 7) was drawing in crowds, nothing could compare to the allure of Lavinia. She was literally a living doll. The museum pulled in about $3,000 a day because of her, and she was also known to sell more than 300 cartes de visite photographs per day. She was a hit—and almost as popular as Thumb had been.

As much as the public adored her, the press revered her. *Harper's Weekly* said of her that "she was all that the most fastidious fancy could desire in a small woman." The *New York Tribune* said, "The woman in miniature . . . has a symmetrical form, and a perfect physical development. She has a full, round, dimpled face, and her fine black eyes sparkle when she becomes interested in conversation." The *New York Sun* was also quite taken with her: "Her dresses are magnificent, being clothed at the rate of $2,000 per outfit, and sparkling with jewels and splendor. Many would deem it a show to see the dress, but dress and contents together are a little ahead of anything which tiny hoops have inclosed [sic] for many a year."

And then there was the third group who couldn't get enough of Lavinia: potential suitors. While many entertained making the diminutive diva their own, there were only two men, at this time, who were in the running. One was her coworker, Commodore Nutt, with whom Barnum was anxious to match her up. She liked

Nutt well enough, but there was never the spark of attraction. She wanted more.

Lavinia had first met Charles Stratton, a.k.a. Tom Thumb, in New York when he was visiting his good friend Barnum at the American Museum. There was no spark then—at least not for Lavinia. The second time she met him, he paid a visit to Lavinia and her mother when they were in Boston in 1861. Lavinia was warming to him at this point, but her mother didn't like Tom at all—and she especially hated the smarmy mustache he'd recently grown.

By this point, Tom Thumb had fallen hard for Lavinia and was determined to win her attention. He had even confided in his pal Barnum about his passion for the petite princess. "Mr. Barnum," he swooned, "that is the most charming little lady I ever saw and I believe she was made on purpose to be my wife." This was in conflict with Barnum's plans for Lavinia, so Barnum tried to talk Tom out of his feelings for Lavinia, even playing up the playboy life that Tom would be tossing away if he got married. Tom was going to make her his wife no matter what. "I have plenty of money," he told Barnum, "and I want to settle down in life."

Another visit with Lavinia, this time in Bridgeport, had Tom utterly convinced—so much so, that this time he asked her to marry him. Lavinia shared the same desire, but, as she had with Barnum when she contracted with him, she played it very cool and took the stance that Thumb wanted her more than she wanted him—no matter what was the real truth. When Tom Thumb proposed to Lavinia, she was aloof, but accepting. Reportedly, she told him that she was having trouble deciding whether or not she should marry him because her mother hated his mustache. He said, "I will cut that off and my ears also if that will induce you to give me an affirmative answer to my question." And she did.

A Valentine's Day wedding had originally been planned, but the lovers, not willing to wait even a few days more, opted instead to set their marriage date for February 10, 1862. Once the engagement was announced, Lavinia's cache at the museum skyrocketed. People were busting down the doors to have a look at the soon-to-be-bride, and she doubled the sales of her autographed cards.

The couple said they married for love—not publicity or money. This could certainly be confirmed when the couple declined Barnum's offer of $15,000 if they would postpone their wedding just another week to make more of the excitement. Barnum acted as a kind of emcee over the festivities, but, shockingly, he did not sell admission tickets. In all, 2,000 attended the nuptials as invited guests, and they included the most stellar celebrities of the time.

The wedding was the social event of the century—quite a contrast to the Civil War, which was in full swing at the time. No expense was spared for the lavish black-tie gala that celebrated the union of the two darlings. They were married in Grace Church, with Minnie Warren and Commodore Nutt acting as attendants.

Almost as impressive as the guest list were the gifts they garnered. Mrs. Astor gave the bride a coral leaf brooch and earrings with diamond centers. Commodore Nutt gifted Lavinia with a diamond ring. Mrs. Greeley presented fourteen silver-plated chafing dishes. The Lennoxes gave the Strattons a porcelain dessert service of eighty-four pieces, and Tiffany & Co. furnished a miniature silver horse and chariot, ornamented with rubies. The Lincolns bestowed a set of gold, silver, and pearl Chinese fire screens.

The day after the wedding, Lavinia and her new husband, along with Minnie Warren and Nutt, left on a honeymoon excursion to tour the world, starting in Philadelphia and then on to Boston. The Strattons went to Washington, D.C., to visit with the Lincolns, who were not able to attend the wedding because of the war, but who were extremely gracious to the couple. Reportedly, President Lincoln was so charmed by Lavinia that he bent himself in half so he could look her in the eyes and said with a smile, "Mrs. Stratton, I wish you much happiness in your union."

After making the rounds in the States, the couple visited with Tom's old friend, Queen Victoria, who, upon taking Lavinia's hand in hers quipped: "It is smaller than an infant's." They spent the better part of the next few years hopping around to various cities in Europe and visiting with royals and dignitaries.

Lavinia was mostly approachable in her life, but she was also something of a snob. She liked to be thought of as someone who was more refined than most. She was also emphatically patriotic; Lavinia's American heritage was very important to her. In her autobiography, she claimed she could date her ancestry "directly back through Richard Warren of the Mayflower company, to William, Earl of Warden, who married Gundera, daughter of William the Conquerer." She concludes by stating: "I fancy that is sufficient to prove my English and American nationality."

Although it is believed that the Strattons had a child, allegedly born December 5, 1863, and who "died" shortly after but had lived long enough to be included in a famous publicity photo, this was not actually the truth. It was nothing more than a promotional stunt because Lavinia, as she later admitted in her autobiography, was unable to have children.

The Strattons continued to enjoy their travels throughout their marriage. They both went back to work temporarily with Barnum in 1881. In 1883, while they were staying away from home, they nearly lost their lives in a hotel fire. Both found it hard to bounce back, especially Lavinia's husband, who made her a widow the following year.

To Lavinia's great surprise, there was no money left when her husband died. She was desperate, destitute, and depressed. It was Barnum who brought her out of her slump. He told her "Keep going, Mrs. Stratton, keep going," and this became her mantra until her own death.

A year after she lost her husband, Lavinia married Count Primo Magri, an Italian midget who had come to America with his brother seeking fame and fortune. They were wed on April 6, 1885. Lavinia went back on tour with her new husband, and the two eventually settled in to life and work at Samuel W. Gumpertz's (see page 88) Lilliputia, also known as Midget City, at Coney Island in Brooklyn, New York.

Lavinia Warren Stratton Magri died of old age in Middleboro in 1919. She was seventy-eight years old.

Jack Earle

a.k.a. "The Texas Giant"
a.k.a. "Jacob Ehrlich"
(1906–1952)

> [Jack Earle] was well proportioned, extremely
> likable, possessed a pleasing personality and
> remarkable intelligence.
>
> —from *Circus: Cinders to Sawdust*

Like many of the performers and impresarios featured in this book, Jack Earle had many talents and diverse interests. His main claim to fame was his sideshow distinction; however, he was also an actor, an accomplished painter and photographer, as well as a published poet.

Jack Earle was born Jacob Ehrlich in 1906 in Denver, Colorado, ironically known as the "mile-high" city. Even though Jack would shoot up to a mile himself—okay, not quite a mile—no one ever expected he would. Like most giants you'll read about here, Ehrlich was not an enormous infant. In fact, he was actually smaller than most. Barely making the slightest impression on the scales at a measly four pounds, it was doubtful that he would even live.

But it wasn't long before he'd show just how sturdy he was. Right away, he began to shoot up in weight and height. Ehrlich was already over six feet tall by the time he was ten years old. At his tallest, he stood eight feet, six and a half inches.

Certainly, he wasn't your average kid or teenager, but still, he could not have predicted the extraordinary opportunities that awaited him in the freak-fascinated world. Ehrlich stood out in his community. Easily noticed because he was a good head and shoulders taller than anyone else in town, soon enough, others became aware of him as well. Hollywood caught Jacob in its sights and he answered the call. He headed to California, changed his name to Jack Earle, and began his first of several careers.

Between 1923 and 1926, Jack Earle reportedly made fifty silent

Jack Earle

comedies, including *A Howling Success* (1923), *A Spooky Romance* (1923), *Hansel and Gretel* (1923), *A Lofty Marriage* (1924), and *Taxi! Taxi!* (1924). *Jack and the Beanstalk* (1924) is the film he is most remembered for.

In the late 1920s, Jack Earle fell from a scaffolding on a film set and nearly died. Even though he survived the fall, he wasn't out of the woods yet. Earle was having trouble with his peripheral vision, which is what had caused him to fall in the first place. Tests revealed that Earle had developed a pituitary gland tumor, which, while benign 99 percent of the time, could still wreak havoc on his system if not cared for. Radiation treatments eventually eradicated the tumor.

Once recovered, Jack decided that his fall and illness were probably signs that he'd been working too hard and that it was time to take a rest. He retired from the movie business when he was still in his twenties and, with the hectic demands of his movie career behind him, enjoyed his life. He moved to El Paso, Texas, where he became a deputy sheriff. He took golf lessons and even worked sporadically as a traveling salesman. Jack enrolled in college to find out what he would do next—then fate intervened.

One day he attended the Ringling Bros. and Barnum & Bailey Circus with some friends. He was easily spotted by showman Clyde Ingalls, who was not about to let the near-eight-foot wonder slip away. Ingalls already had a tall man, Jack (Jim) Tarver as part of his ensemble, but two would certainly boost business. Ingalls made Earle a generous offer. Jack left school and commenced the career that would carry him through a fair portion of his remaining life.

For the next fourteen years, the "Tallest Man in the World" (Tarver was only seven feet, ten inches tall) toured the country and the world with the famed circus. Eventually, the extensive traveling grew tiring and by the early 1940s, Jack was ready to retire from the circus and make a life for himself enjoying hobbies he now had the time to pursue and perfect.

In every sense of the word, Jack Earle was a renaissance man. In addition to continuing to make his living on the road as a traveling salesman, he wrote and published a book of poetry, *The Long Shadows*. He was also a renowned painter, sculptor, and award-winning photographer.

Texas Giant Jack Earle died at home in El Paso, in 1952, having packed several lifetimes into just forty-six years.

Jóhann Petursson

a.k.a. "Jóhann Svarfdælingur"
a.k.a. "The Icelandic Giant"
a.k.a. "The Hollywood Giant"
a.k.a. "The Tallest Man in the World"
(1913–1984)

> O! It is excellent
> To have a giant's strength, but it is tyrannous
> To use it like a giant.
> —From Shakespeare's *Measure for Measure*

Iceland Giant Jóhann Petursson was a "gentle giant," who, besides his work with the sideshow, also made films. Unlike Jack Earle (see page 26), however, his Hollywood career came after he earned renown as a circus performer.

Jóhann was born in Davlik, Iceland, on February 9, 1913, as Jóhann Svarfdælingur. He was third in a brood of nine, but was the only one in his family known to be so tall. At his full-grown height, close to nine feet, he was the tallest Icelander ever known. For a while, until Alton giant Robert Wadlow (see page 33) shot up past him, Jóhann even enjoyed a reputation as the "Tallest Man Alive."

Petursson was so big, it required three people to measure him for clothing. By the time Jóhann was twenty years old, when he reportedly stopped growing, he stood an astounding eight feet, eight inches tall and weighed 425 pounds. Jóhann wore size 84 shoes, European. In American measurements, that's about a size 24. (The to-date Tallest Man Robert Wadlow wore a size 37.)

Growing up, the personable Jóhann had many friends in school. As an adult, he was equally well liked in the town, but that didn't mean he was employable. Because he couldn't fit into any of the tiny shops, there wasn't much work the giant could really do. Even in school he couldn't comfortably squeeze himself behind the "child-size" desks. The town was too small for his mammoth proportions and he realized he would soon have to leave the comfort he had always known if he wished to earn a living. It wouldn't be until tragedy struck that Peturrson would get on with his life, however.

On June 2, 1934, just after midnight, a devastating earthquake hit Davlik. A reported 6.2 to 6.3 on the Richter scale, it was the biggest earthquake ever recorded in the region. Remarkably, no lives were reported lost; however, the buildings and businesses in the town were all but destroyed. Even the crops in the fields were affected. It was difficult enough for Jóhann to find work before; now that the town was essentially leveled, he had no choice but to leave home and find his own way.

Jóhann eventually arrived in Denmark. There, he learned something that never would have occurred to him within the comfy confines of his hometown. He discovered that simply by exhibiting himself, he could make a living, and a healthy one at that. And if he could pull in such an enormous take in Denmark, who knew what riches awaited throughout the other countries of Europe? Jóhann signed up with a traveling circus and toured the Continent for the next several years.

In 1939 when World War II began, Jóhann was in Copenhagen. Europe was a mess, to be sure, and he was all but trapped in Copenhagen until after the war. When it became safe to travel again, Jóhann returned to Iceland and traveled around his home country for a few years. He headed for the United States in 1948.

When he arrived in the States, at thirty-five years of age, Jóhann signed on with Ringling Bros. and Barnum & Bailey Circus, which was showcasing such beloved acts as the Doll Family (see page 14). There wasn't a tall man in the ensemble at the time, so management eagerly welcomed Jóhann into the fold. The gentle giant was as beloved as he was famous, and he enjoyed his time with the circus as much as his audiences—and bosses—loved having him there.

In 1950, Hollywood called. The producers of a B-movie called *Prehistoric Women* had a role for "Guadi the Giant," and Jóhann, being the most prominent, visible, and essentially only giant working at that time, was instantly wooed for the part. The film was a silly account of a tribe of self-sufficient man-hating prehistoric babes who realize they're eventually going to need men to help them continue the race. They capture a bunch of men, who eventually take

Petursson Giant

over. Eventually, the women and men unite to protect each other from greater evils, namely, the evil, angry Guadi. *Prehistoric Women* is also notable as the film debut of 1950s sexpot Jayne Mansfield.

This wasn't Jóhann's first performance on the big screen. During the war, in Denmark, he played a small part in a black-and-white film called *Hjertetyven* (1943). This little-known film was all but obscure at this point; however, fervent B-movie fans are not quick to forget Jóhann's performance in *Prehistoric Women* (1950). Bmoviecentral.com describes Guadi as "a brute that wanders around, kidnaps women, and generally terrorizes everyone he comes across." Quite a stretch for such a gentle, mild-mannered guy.

In the 1960s, Jóhann retired to Gibsonton, Florida, planning to live out his days in the company of fellow giant Al Tomaini and his "Half-Girl" wife Jeanie (see page 205), Frank "the Human Tripod" Lentini (see page 100), and other retired performers who called Gibsonton home. He essentially stayed out of the spotlight except for a short stint for Ward Hall (see page 171) in 1973 at the Smithsonian Museum in Washington, D.C. After that, he returned to peaceful obscurity, determined to stay there—that is, until Hollywood beckoned again.

In 1980, Jóhann had a small role in the film *Carny*, which starred Jodie Foster, Gary Busey, and Robbie Robertson, and also featured fellow Gibsonton residents Percilla "Monkey Girl" Bejano and her husband, Emmett (see page 196).

In 1981, Jóhann was featured in *Being Different*, a documentary-slash-tribute about modern-day freaks and their place in the world, which also featured Bob "the Man with Two Faces" Melvin and Jeanie Tomaini.

By 1982, Jóhann had had enough of the American way, and he returned to Iceland to finally retire. At sixty-nine years old, he was incredibly aged for a giant, and time had taken a fierce toll on his hulking build. No longer properly able to care for himself, Jóhann entered a nursing home, where he died two years later on November 26, 1984. He's buried in his beloved Davlik, but far from forgotten. Reportedly, a museum there houses many of Jóhann's belongings, which, more than twenty years after his death, remain a source of constant curiosity.

Robert Wadlow
a.k.a. "The Gentle Giant"
(1918–1940)

> He was not a circus freak as a lot of people may
> think. He was an intelligent, caring man.
>> —spoken by a representative of Wadlow's,
>> as reported in Robert Bogdan's *Freak Show*

Robert Pershing Wadlow spent less than a year of his short life with the circus, and unlike just about every other person in this book, he fully detested the idea of the institution and any minute he had to spend in it. To this day, his surviving relatives vehemently fight against associating Wadlow with the circus and the image of "freak show." It isn't at all surprising; Wadlow entered the business as an act of desperation and at a time when the heyday of the sideshow was long past its prime. By the end of the 1930s, sideshows were no longer considered respectable venues for family entertainment, but exploitive freak fests. Not everyone at that time shared that perception, but more individuals opposed the freak show than supported it.

Of course, like every other act in this book, Robert was much more than just a giant. There was considerable substance behind the spectacle. Aside from his size, *normal* isn't exactly a word one could pin on Robert. He was actually quite remarkable. He was kind hearted, spiritual, and highly intelligent. More than sixty years after his death, he continues to be remembered as a gentle man who did what he could to squeeze himself into his pint-sized world. Also, he holds on to his title of "tallest man of all time" in the *Guinness Book of World Records*.

Harold and Addie Johnson Wadlow were first-time parents when Robert was born in Alton, Illinois, on February 22, 1918. Like most giants, Robert was completely normal at birth. He weighed in at eight pounds, six ounces, and measured about fifteen inches. His parents were both of average size. There had never been a history of

Robert Wadlow

giantism in the family, and therefore there was no indication at all that Robert would grow to such epic proportions.

Then he shot up, and quickly at that. By his first birthday, Robert was already a whopping forty-four pounds, about the size of an average third-grader. At five, he was as big as an average seventeen-year-old at just over five feet, six inches tall. By the time he was nine years old, Robert was six feet, two inches tall.

The Wadlows had four more children: Helen, Betty, Eugene, and Harold Jr. None were giants. Obviously, therefore, Robert garnered much attention, and not just from his family. Throughout his childhood, showmen hounded the Wadlows to persuade Robert to tour as an act, but Robert's parents turned down all offers. They wanted him to have a life experience as normal as possible, and Robert was in full agreement with this. That is, he was at this time.

Robert lived like a normal kid. He went to school; he collected stamps. He liked to take pictures; he even became a Boy Scout. Of course, he had to have his uniform custom made: At age thirteen when he signed up with the Scouts, he was already seven feet, four inches tall. (To put this in perspective, consider that Shaquille O'Neal stands at a mere seven feet, one inch and weighs 340 pounds.)

By the age of sixteen, Robert had become the largest human male who ever lived. Aside from this, everything else about him, physically, was absolutely normal. He enjoyed perfect health and had no restrictions on what he could do. The only physical thing that ever bothered him were his enormous size-37 feet.

Robert attended Alton High School in the early 1930s and slipped in to the experience with the same gentle ease he had called upon throughout his life. He participated in several activities and was even advertising manager of the school yearbook. Upon his 1936 graduation, the ever-impressive Robert was awarded a college scholarship. By the time he was college aged, he was already eight feet, four inches tall and carried nearly 400 pounds on his lean frame—and still growing.

Robert had plans to become a lawyer, and the scholarship would have helped that pursuit tremendously, but, unfortunately, Robert never got his degree. In fact, he spent little time in college. The one-time ease Robert had always felt with his Lilliputian world and friends and acquaintances was gone, and he felt something he had never known before when he was away at school: small. Well, maybe on the inside. On the outside, he felt like a cramped whale in a pond of indifferent strangers. The new struggles proved to be too frustrating for him. By now, Robert had reached his full height of eight feet, eleven inches, and 490 pounds.

Robert had always worked. As a youngster, he had sold magazines. He always looked out for himself and enjoyed his self-sufficiency. Moving back home and living off his parents was not a comfortable option for him. He needed to be productive, and there was only one way he knew how.

In 1937, Ringling Brothers Circus came calling again. This time, he didn't refuse, though he had several conditions. As Robert Bogdan relates, Wadlow made many restrictions in his contract. He wasn't going to travel the country or the world as part of a "sideshow"; he insisted upon being part of the main attraction. Bogdan writes that Wadlow "would appear only at the engagements at Madison Square Garden and the Boston Garden . . . two times a day for three minutes each . . . he would not appear in the sideshow but in the center ring."

Also written into Wadlow's contract was that he would not condone any "tricks when it came to his height." He would be costumed in his typical attire of a conservative business suit; elevated shoes, top hats, and any kind of trick photography to make him look taller was strictly forbidden.

This was not a highlight in Robert's life or for his family; most accounts of his life written by sources close to him omit his time with the circus entirely. Needless to say, he didn't expend much time with the circus. It did give him another opportunity, however.

As Robert was more visible than ever before, more people had access to him. The International Shoe Company courted Robert to work for them, and he jumped at the chance. In 1940, Robert left the freak show and, with his dad, toured the country as an ambassador for the International Shoe Company. In one year, Robert and his dad made about 800 appearances in an astounding forty-one states. Together they traveled about 300,000 miles.

Aside from now having a steady paycheck that still involved people gawking at him but at least more respectably, Robert did enjoy one perk: The International Shoe Company provided him free shoes. This was awesome because Robert's size-37 shoes generally cost him upward of $100—a pretty steep investment in the 1930s. Robert's feet usually gave him trouble, however. Their amazing size made it uncomfortable to stuff them into shoes, no matter how customized. It wasn't uncommon for him to be afflicted with blisters and other foot problems.

On July 4, 1940, while appearing in Manistee, Michigan, Robert's blistered feet flared into a full-fledged infection. He immediately saw a doctor, who recommended that he stay off his feet. The doctor's plan was to confine Robert to a bed in the hospital, but no bed was large enough to accommodate him. Instead, Robert checked in to a hotel, where it is doubtful he could have received sufficient medical attention. Still, doctors tried everything in their makeshift medical facility, including surgery and blood transfusions. It would not be enough.

On July 15, 1940, at 1:30 A.M., Robert Pershing Wadlow died in his sleep. He was just twenty-two years old.

Robert was adored across the country and any town would have been proud to host his funeral, but Robert's body was sent back to his beloved hometown of Alton. All the local businesses closed during his funeral, which attracted an astounding 40,000 mourners. Robert was buried in Upper Alton Cemetery in a thousand-pound casket that required twelve pallbearers to hoist. The casket was encased in a vault of concrete to protect Robert from curious body snatchers. In an effort to protect Robert's memory from being tarnished with a "freak" stigma, his family burned all of his possessions shortly after his death so that no one would have the opportunity to collect or sell them.

In 1985, a life-sized bronze statue of Wadlow was erected in Alton, but not before a controversial battle waged. Those who typically opposed putting people who were "different" on display were against the statue, because it was a permanent reminder of that type of perceived exploitation. The group in favor of the statue was divided between those who remembered him and wanted to pay tribute to their giant and those who were working acts at the time, including Otis Jordan (see page 83), the "Frog Boy," whose very livelihood was being threatened at the time by those who thought they were protecting him. So, in a twist of irony, those who represented the life Robert's family never wanted for him stepped up to the plate and helped win the cause. The statue still stands at the Southern Illinois Dental School in Alton.

Chang Woo Gow

a.k.a. "Chang Yu Sang"
a.k.a. "The Chinese Giant"
a.k.a. "The Magic Giant"
(1841–1893)

> I don't want to live—
> I want to love first,
> And live incidentally.
>
> —Zelda Fitzgerald, letter to F. Scott
> Fitzgerald, 1919

Every giant has something that sets him or her apart from others. Like the other giants featured, Chang Woo Gow was extremely personable and intelligent—speaking his native Chinese as well as being fluent in English, French, German, Spanish, and Japanese. He was also noted as being extremely "gentle," a distinction given to most if not all the giants here. He adored the finer things in life and always adorned himself in costumes of pure Chinese silk and satin and the finest furs and skins. He donned jewelry of all kinds and was especially fond of ebony and pearls.

In addition, Chang, the Chinese giant, was deeply devoted to his wife. Some believe that if not for this devotion, he would have lived much longer than he did.

Born in Fy-Chow, a province of Canton in China, in 1841, Chang

THE ASHLEIGH HOTEL

Chang Woo Gow

arrived into an already large family. Records do not reveal whether he was an oversized baby, but we do know that he was not the only giant in his family. A sister reportedly "dwarfed" Chang at eight feet, four inches tall to his seven feet, nine inches.

No documentation exists of Chang's childhood, or of how and when he decided to exhibit himself; therefore, no one knows whether he decided on his own to make his living in such a way or if he was scouted out. Reports say he was an instant sensation, both for his height and his personality, and he was the frequent guest of monarchs and other dignitaries. He was a personal favorite of the Prince and Princess of Wales, who were avid fans of human curiosities. When Chang visited with them in the 1860s, they asked him to paint his name in one of their rooms in Chinese characters, and he dutifully obliged. Chang painted the characters at a height of over ten feet from the floor.

In the 1870s, Chang went into a period of semi-retirement. While he continued his travels, he cut his exhibition schedule in order to enjoy the cities he visited, Vienna, Berlin, and St. Petersburg. In that period, he also traveled to Australia. Here, he met his darling wife, Catherine Stanley. Some accounts say that Chang's wife was a Chinese woman named King-Foo, which means "the fair lily." This was not entirely incorrect. When Catherine traveled with Chang, she donned the traditional attire of a Chinese woman and was called King-Foo; however, she was not by any stretch of the imagination Chinese. Catherine was actually born in Liverpool, and when she was still a small child, her family moved to Australia.

Shortly after they married, the newlyweds moved to China to be close to Chang's family. They didn't stay long. All the money that Chang had accumulated throughout his years on exhibit was starting to dwindle. The cost of living was part of it, but Chang's generous-to-a-fault nature and desire to give all his money away to anyone who needed or wanted it—and his proclivity for the finer things of course—also played a major role. Soon, it was time to hit the road again.

In 1878, Chang came out of retirement. He exhibited himself throughout Europe, starting in Paris. By this time, he had grown even taller: He was now just over eight feet tall and a svelte 400 pounds. In addition to his wife, Chang also toured around with a three-foot-tall dwarf friend named Chung Mow, who popped into many of Chang's publicity shots. Often, when Chang was exhibited in Europe, he would also be featured with another giant, Henrik Berstaad, who was, by most accounts, two inches shorter than Chang.

In 1880, Chang wanted to retire again, and this time it was for real. He and his wife bought property in Bournemouth, England, between the seaside and the town. They had been many places in their travels, but they had never fallen in love with any place like they had with Bournemouth. They settled into their brand new home with their two young sons, Edwin and Ernest, and Chang made a living running side businesses from his home. The tea, embroidered Oriental linens, curios, and crafts he sold provided him with enough income to not have to worry about going back on the road.

Retirement was bliss, but paradise had its limits. One of the other reasons that the couple had moved to this quaint village was that Bournemouth was a place where people came to if they had tuberculosis. The climate was conducive to making the afflicted more comfortable and also to extending their lives. Catherine had been diagnosed with TB before Chang's retirement but was still very strong for several years. Then, in 1893, Catherine's health took a sharp turn toward decline. Late that summer, she succumbed.

By all reports, Chang was healthy and robust until his wife passed away. Then, four months later, he died. Some say that he, too, had tuberculosis, and it finally caught up with him when his resistance was completely worn down by the stress caused by his wife's death. More romantic assertions, however, cite the cause of his death as the actual loss of his wife. All who knew him recognized how desperately devoted he was to her and swore that what killed Chang was a broken heart. Of course, it must also be noted that giants do not typically live long lives; at the time of his passing, Chang was fifty-two—almost old for a giant.

Chang was buried on November 8, 1893, in Bournemouth, in the same grave as his wife. In respect of his wishes, the service was very small for a one-time world-class celebrity, with only fifty or so mourners permitted to attend.

Today, Chang's Bournemouth home has been converted into a hotel. The hoteliers of the Ashleigh Hotel, which it is now called, provide historic tours for visitors as well as access to historic documents and photographs left behind by Chang's family when they sold the house.

BOUND FOR STARDOM

Rosa and Josepha Blazek

a.k.a. "The Bohemian Twins"
a.k.a. *"Le pygopage du Théâtre de l'âge Gaité"*
(1878–1922)

> I'm gonna have to level with you. Siamese twins
> ain't the easiest sell I've ever had.
> —Morty O'Reilly (Seymour Cassel), *Stuck on You* (2003)

Of all the scandal that surrounds Siamese twins and their sex lives, Rosa and Josepha Blazek certainly suffered the most. Although minor scandals erupted when male Siamese twins like Chang and Eng Bunker (see page 46) and the Tocci brothers (see page 71) wanted to wed, eventually the heat cooled and these male twins were able to live their lives with their wives and several children. This would never be the case for the Bohemian Siamese twins, however; even when one of them had a baby out of wedlock, they were still refused the opportunity to wed.

On the night of January 20, 1878, twin daughters were born to a young couple in the rural village of Skerychov, Bohemia, in Czechoslovakia. That would have been well and good if they had been born

Rosa and Josepha Blazek

separate, but these girls were pygopagus twins, born connected at the hip.

The new parents, who were highly superstitious folk, turned to a local witch to find out why this had happened to their family and what they could do to rectify the problem. The witch recommended an incredibly cruel plan of action, no doubt seeing that the best solution to the Blazeks' problem was to eradicate it completely. She told the parents to withhold food from the baby girls for eight days. Remarkably, the girls survived. The witch informed the Blazeks this meant that the connected girls were absolutely meant to be as they were and the reason for their conjoined condition would show itself in time.

The infants grew into healthy, intelligent, and remarkably personable girls. Despite their unusual stature—or perhaps because of it—Rosa and Josepha were hugely popular in their small village. Word soon spread outside the village. They were so much talked about that showmen came from far and wide, paying constant visits to the middle-of-nowhere farm and hoping to land the girls as attractions in their museums and traveling exhibits.

Mrs. Blazek, as suspicious as she was superstitious, would not agree to let anyone take her girls and put them on display, no matter how ridiculously abundant the payoff. She was so adamant about it that when the girls were thirteen, she traveled with her daughters to see a physician in Paris, who reportedly had successfully separated conjoined twins many times before.

Upon a thorough examination, the doctor said the girls could not be separated and that doing so would mean death for at least one and perhaps both twins. The girls were thrilled. They didn't want to be separated. They felt as one person together. But more than that, they saw a way to escape the small village where they lived. To see the world and fame and fortune that would be theirs only if they remained as one and not two . . .

Even though the girls were still very young, they were determined. They convinced their mother to let them stay in Paris, and she finally relented. The Blazek twins landed a manager and began their life in the spotlight.

Rosa and Josepha learned to sing and to play the xylophone. They mastered the violin and became famous for their duets. They spent the better part of the 1890s touring Europe, but they never made it to the States. By the turn of the twentieth century, the novelty had worn off. Without a showman like Barnum to back them and keep them fresh, the public interest in them simply vanished—that is, until a scandal made them famous again.

Now grown women, the bond of constant sisterhood became strained—metaphorically speaking. Even when very young, it was blatantly obvious that Rosa and Josepha were two separate girls—their own person each of them—just connected with bone and tissue to another. They looked alike but they weren't exactly identical in appearance: Rosa was taller and stronger than Josepha, as is quite common in conjoined twins.

The twins liked different foods and drinks. They were never hungry or thirsty at the same time. One might sleep while the other was awake. Rosa was apparently quick witted and charming; Josepha, dim witted and dull. And though they shared many sensations, there were many they did not; sex, they insisted, fell under the category of "didn't share."

Rosa was suspected of being the more sexually active of the two, but both clung fast to empty proclamations of virtue. But as the shape of their shared body began to change, there was no way to deny any longer that they had been intimate with a man.

There's no proof of Josepha's having any sexual dalliances. It was suspected that the sisters shared genitals, but the truth was they merely shared an anus; each had her own vagina and therefore each had accountability when it came to what she did with it. Rosa gave birth to a baby boy, Franzl, at the Prague General Hospital, on April 17, 1910, through natural means. There was no sense in denying it anymore, so Rosa admitted her liaison.

Instead of being treated as an exciting and marvelous medical miracle, the birth was an outrage. It raised all kinds of unpleasant imagery in the heads of pure and virtuous folk, which actually backfired for everyone. Instead of having the opportunity to do the "right" thing—the father of the boy very much wanted to marry his paramour and legitimize his son—the law, and the family, vehemently opposed the union, citing bigamy and no doubt envisioning all kinds of other immoralities.

It has been said that this pregnancy and birth scandal was the straw that broke the camel's back; after this, apparently all they ever wished for was to be separated. The differences between the two sisters had become so pronounced that it was nearly impossible for them to live together anymore (not that this was an option).

In 1922, the twins joined their brother who had moved to the United States several years earlier. Not long after beginning their new life in Chicago, Josepha, the weaker of the twins, developed jaundice. On March 30, 1922, she passed away. Remarkably, Rosa was so strong, she was able to fend off the grim reaper for three more days, holding on until April 2, 1922. There is a rumor that Rosa begged to be separated from her sister after her death. Certainly there would have been time; but their brother, who had more power over their lives than a brother should, expressly forbade it.

Chang and Eng Bunker

a.k.a. "The Siamese Twins"
a.k.a. "The Double Siamese Boys"
a.k.a. "The United Brothers"
(1811–1874)

> All your strength is in your union.
> All your danger is in discord;
> Therefore be at peace henceforward,
> And as brothers live together.
>> —Henry Wadsworth Longfellow,
>> from "The Song of Hiawatha"

Coming on to the scene in the late 1820s, these Siamese twin brothers may very well have been the first "sideshow" act. However, if they weren't the first human exhibit, they were certainly the

Chang and Eng Bunker

first international sensation. To the present day, their popularity abounds. Two novels have been written about them, each taking the point of view of one of the brothers. There's also been a musical, though it has yet to find its way to Broadway.

In reality, the brothers were barely bound. They shared a kind of "hyphen" between them—a five-inch-long, three-inch-wide strip of cartilage, in which their shared liver resided. Otherwise, all their parts were individual. So why couldn't they be separated? The reasons were many, including that medicine was not quite advanced enough at the time to ensure a successful separation. When they were alive, there were no CAT scans; it was impossible for doctors to know exactly which body parts the twins shared. While most guessed it was likely just a liver, in the days before organ transplants, it's certain that one of the brothers would have died during the separation. Also, the bond between the brothers was more than physical, which has at least something to do with their not wanting to be separated.

Born in a houseboat sixty miles west of Siam (today Thailand) on May 11, 1811, ChangChun and Eng-in scared the bejesus out of the midwife who delivered them. In fact, the whole village was frantic. Even the king of Siam, Rama II, was terrified that the existence of the boys signified a very bad omen for the entire country; he wanted them executed at once. The king relented, clearly, but he was still insistent that they at least be separated. The ghoulish methods suggested, glowing hot wires and a saw, were unthinkable to their mother, Nok, and she pleaded with the king to leave them be. Whatever she did worked. Nok named her sons Chang and Eng, which meant "left" and "right."

Nok was a Chinese-Malaysian woman who, at the time she had Chang and Eng, had already given birth to four other perfectly formed and healthy children. Their father, Ti-eye, was fully Chinese and was a fairly successful fisherman. As the boys grew from infants into healthy and robust children, they became more and more accepted. Initially only able to stand face to face, Nok had trained the twins to stretch their connecting fiber so that they could stand side by side. This gave them much more mobility and allowed them to help out with the family, which was a very good thing because the brood grew to a whopping nine children.

When the twins were eight years old, a cholera epidemic swept through the village. Ti-eye and five of the other children in the family died. Without their main provider, the family became destitute, but, luckily, Chang and Eng were eager and able to help out. The boys worked for their mother and surviving siblings, selling duck eggs and coconut oil at the harbor.

As the years passed, the twins became more and more famous. They were even summoned by the king, who no longer wanted to execute them, only to meet them, when they were sixteen years old. Word quickly spread outside their country and it was only a matter of time before they were discovered.

In the late 1820s, British merchant Robert Hunter was exploring Siam when he encountered the unusual, connected young men, now seventeen years old. Observing how active they were, he saw great potential for financial gain. He and his partner, Abel Coffin, struck a deal with Nok to take the boys to America to become performers. They offered her $3,000, including a huge chunk of the profits. (Some accounts say it was merely $500, but it's hard to believe that Nok, who had always been sensible and protective of her sons, would let them go so cheaply.) She agreed, but the decision was not just hers to make. The men had to get clearance from the king, who was hesitant to let what he perceived as national treasures go. It took him nearly three years to relent.

In 1829, the conjoined boys and their managers docked in Boston. This was the beginning of a whirlwind tour of the United States and the world. Captain Coffin dubbed them as "Siamese Double Boys" and taught them to speak English. It didn't take long for them to become a worldwide sensation, except in France. French officials feared the boys would cause severe maternal impression. They worried that if pregnant women saw the show, birth defects and deformities resembling Chang and Eng's condition would result when the observer's own babies were born.

At first, Chang and Eng had no act to speak of; it had never occurred to anyone that they needed one. Indeed, they were so unusual, Coffin thought it would be sufficient for them to just stand and let people ogle them, and answer questions when asked. This grew tedious for audiences and performers alike, and soon Chang and Eng spruced up their act on their own. In addition to the requisite question-and-answer period, the men performed somersaults and other acrobatic maneuvers. They also demonstrated how freakishly strong they were by lifting improbably heavy objects.

The older Chang and Eng became, the more their distinct and quite different personalities began to emerge. In addition to being an inch taller than Eng, Chang was loud and boisterous, while Eng proved to be more introspective and intellectual. Eventually, Chang would become a heavy drinker and a malcontent; Eng would lose considerable sums of money because of his passion for gambling. But that wouldn't be till much later.

When the twins began working with Coffin, he paid each brother $10 per month and covered all their expenses. Two years later, they received raises to $50 per month, again with expenses included. That may seem like okay money for the time, but their act typically brought in upward of $1,000 at a clip; it's not hard to see that they were being cheated. They saw it, too, and as soon as they could legally emancipate themselves from Coffin, that's just what they did. When they turned twenty-one, the boys sent the exploitive Coffin on his way and were at last able to keep all the profits they reeled in for themselves, which was going to be quite a sum. For each show they performed, they charged an admission of 50 cents per person; it didn't take long before they were able to amass a fortune of more than $60,000.

Within a decade of enjoying international stardom, the traveling and the lifestyle started to wear on the twins. On the advice of a physician and friend, Dr. James Calloway, they took a much-needed vacation. In a small town in North Carolina, they not only found the rest they had been craving, they also found something they hadn't enjoyed since they left Siam: a permanent home. Chang and Eng decided to quit show business, settle into a more quiet life in the sleepy town, and open a country store. When that failed, they didn't head back to the sideshow. They had no interest. Instead, they turned their efforts to tobacco farming, buying, in parcels, a 1,000-acre farm.

Once they retired, everything began falling into place. Over the course of the next several years, they became naturalized citizens. They changed their last name to "Bunker" to anchor them to their new country. They each found love.

In the early 1840s, Chang and Eng met Wilkesboro sisters Adelaide (Addie) and Sarah (who was sometimes called Sally) Yates. Some accounts speculate that it was really Chang and Addie who fell in love, but Eng and Sarah were talked into going along with things, and over time, both couples became, well, inseparable.

Of course, whomever was in love with whom hardly mattered to the townspeople—and to the Yates girls' family. When the couples announced their plans to marry, speculation of the indecency of the unions and all the sexual ramifications that would occur as a result of it nearly drove them apart. But the romantic bonds were strong.

In an attempt to assuage the scandal, Chang and Eng traveled to see a New England doctor who was famous for such separations. They didn't go through with it. Most accounts say the reason for this was that the tearful fiancées bounded into the hospital and put a stop to things; other accounts report that there was no way both twins were going to survive the separation and it was refused when they asked for it.

On April 13, 1843, in a double ceremony at the Yates family home, the marriages became official. Nine months later, Addie gave birth to a daughter; six days after that, Sarah also gave birth to a daughter. Between them, Chang and Eng would sire a brood of twenty-one children—eleven for Chang and ten for Eng—and not a one born as "two."

Chang and Eng set up two households for their families. The men spent three nights with one wife and family, three with the other. They lived this way for years.

The couples enjoyed their farmers' lives, but the increasing number of mouths to feed meant they needed more money. Besides, the twins missed the showbiz life. Before they retired, they had met Barnum; now, in the late 1850s, they joined up with the famous showman once again. They ended up touring with Barnum and picked up considerable money doing so. By the time they took another respite, the brothers had amassed some $35,000 more, and even owned a considerable number of slaves.

After the Civil War was over, the Bunkers' comfortable fortune had trickled down to less than a third of what it had been. Many accounts say this was the beginning of ugly confrontations between the twins. Their families stopped getting along. One account says that the money was unequally divided before the war, giving the Chang Bunkers more assets and the Eng Bunkers more slaves. After the Civil War and abolition, that would render the Eng Bunkers' assets essentially worthless. At this time the brothers also started to develop their less-than-desirable habits. Chang took up the bottle; Eng took up cards.

By 1868, conditions were so bad between the brothers that they headed to Europe to seek separation surgery, each with a daughter in tow. Some accounts say they were also touring while they were there. Whatever the case, they returned to the States in 1870 when war broke out between Prussia and France, and not only were they still brotherly bound, but Chang had suffered a debilitating stroke on the ship voyage back to the States. Eng was not affected by the stroke, but for the rest of their lives, Chang would be a huge burden to him.

A couple of years after they returned to the States, Chang developed a case of chronic bronchitis that plagued him till he died. On a January night in 1874, Chang passed away. Eng, understandably, was absolutely terrified. A doctor had been called to try and sever the pair, but he arrived on the scene much too late. Within a few hours of Chang's death, Eng's followed. An autopsy revealed that Chang died from a blood clot to the brain. There's no definitive way to discern how Eng died, and many have speculated that he died of fright. It's most likely that he bled to death. The world-famous Siamese twins were sixty-three years old.

Initially, in fear of grave looters and overly curious anatomy students, Chang and Eng were buried in the basement of the Chang Bunker home. They rested there for two years before being buried at the White Plains Baptist Church. When Addie died, she joined them there; Sally did not. She was buried on the grounds of the home she shared with her husband.

Before Chang and Eng were laid to rest, a plaster cast was made of their upper bodies. Also, following an autopsy, their shared livers were removed for scientific study. Both the cast and the liver are on permanent display at the Mütter Museum, at the College of Physicians, in Philadelphia, Pennsylvania.

Margaret and Mary Gibb
a.k.a. "The American Siamese Twins"
(1912–1967)

> They are two of the nicest people I have ever met
> in my life.
> —Dr. Frank Lahey, a surgeon who twice operated on the Gibb twins

Contemporaries of the more famous, and wild, Hilton twins (see page 105), Mary and Margaret Gibb were the resident "nice girls" in the conjoined twins milieu. Wholesome as vanilla ice cream, they would never have been caught up in a sex scandal like the Blazek twins (see page 56).

Like many Siamese twins, Mary and Margaret Gibb were very different—physically, intellectually, and emotionally. Mary was plump, but also easygoing and carefree; thin Margaret was reportedly high-strung, nervous, and even shrill. Mary was four feet, eight inches; Margaret was four-foot-ten. Reportedly, Mary's complexion was slightly darker than Margaret's, which seems odd but must be believed on faith if at all because it is impossible to discern from their black-and-white photos that exist.

The goodie-goodie Gibb girls were born in Holyoke, Massachusetts, on May 20, 1912, to John and Margaret (née Lawrence) Gibb. The Gibbs were respectable members of their community, so it was a great relief when news came about the double birth that Margaret, the mother, had survived it. Many believed she was the only woman in the United States to ever have survived the birth of conjoined twins, but, of course, this is false. Millie-Christine McKoy (see page 64) were born in 1851, to their mother Monemia McKoy, who lived a long time afterward.

Whatever the parents felt about their children being connected, they realized that the Lord had his reasons, and they were adamantly opposed to having the girls surgically separated. For one, the procedure could be fatal for one or both girls. Additionally, from a very young age, the girls themselves expressed a desire to remain just the way they were.

Another thing the parents passionately tried to prevent was to subject their girls to any kind of public ridicule, especially from the roving eyes of showmen in search of the next big act. Thus, for the first few years of their lives, the girls were a sensation only in medical communities. Also, to protect them from the cruel tendencies of other children, the girls were homeschooled by their mother and by tutors.

Of course, Mom couldn't shield them forever. As the girls grew older, they began to make their own decisions. One of these was their career choice. When Mary and Margaret were about fifteen years old, they entered the world of show business, not in the sideshow, but in vaudeville. Their song-and-dance sister act made them instantly famous. Although their parents were opposed to the girls making themselves public at first, they were not about to leave their precious ones in the hands of strangers. They wouldn't hire a guardian, they would tour with the girls themselves. By this time, there was another addition to the Gibb clan, a girl named Dorothy.

The Gibbs traveled throughout the United States, and the girls pulled in enough revenue that John Gibb no longer had to worry about supporting his family. In 1930, the Gibb girls embarked upon a colossal European tour, during which they were guests of royalty and dignitaries throughout the Continent. Common folk and VIPs alike embraced the singing sisters in Paris, Brussels, Zurich, and hundreds more cities.

By the time the Great Depression rolled around, vaudeville was essentially gasping its last breath. The economy was only part of the reason; the advent of "talkies" (motion pictures), which provided people with more economical entertainment, essentially drove the last nail into the vaudeville coffin.

One form of live entertainment, however, was not affected too much by the Depression: the circus. Traveling shows, which required very little in terms of cost, thrived. Thus, in 1934, the Gibb sisters signed on with Ringling Bros. and Barnum & Bailey Circus. In 1938, they switched over to appear with the Cole Brothers, then switched back between one and the other for the next several years, a practice not uncommon with sideshow performers looking to leverage their salaries.

By 1941, the Gibbs were tired of always being on the run. It was time to settle down. In 1942, they moved back to Holyoke and opened the Mary-Margaret Gift Shoppe. In this quaint little venue, they sold cards, vases, novelties, and children's and baby clothes made with their own hands. The store was very successful and they kept it open until 1949.

Now retired completely, at the age of thirty-seven, Mary and Margaret Gibb became hermits. They never ventured out except for church. They spent their time holed up together in the house they shared, knitting and, when the medium became available, watching television. In the mid-1960s, Mary and Margaret moved in with their mother (their father had already passed away) and their younger sister.

For the most part, the Gibb girls enjoyed good health—at least Mary did. They had undergone two surgeries together, surgeries that were performed on Margaret. There was a bladder stone in 1946. In 1953, a more serious surgery was performed. Margaret had developed a fibroid tumor that needed to be removed. Otherwise, there was nothing wrong with them—not for a few more years at least.

In 1966, Margaret contracted cancer of the bladder. When the diagnosis was made, it had not yet spread to Mary. Because they shared a circulatory system, it was essential to Mary's survival that she be separated from her sister. But for Mary, this was not an option. She just couldn't bear the idea that she wouldn't be with her sister—her other half—so Mary refused separation.

The cancer spread throughout both bodies, and in June 1967, they died—first Margaret, followed by Mary two minutes later. They were fifty-four years old. The Gibb twins are buried in the Forestdale Cemetery in their hometown of Holyoke. Their tombstone bears this simple inscription: "This is the way we were born, this is the way we want to live."

Daisy and Violet Hilton

a.k.a. "San Antonio's Siamese Twins"
a.k.a. "The Texas Twins"
(1908–1969)

> Joined together as we are, there could be no such thing for either of us as a private life. . . . We are believed to share identical thrills, pains and even diseases. The truth is that we are as different in our reactions as day and night. I Violet, often weep over something which makes my sister chuckle. I had whooping cough a year and a half before Daisy. We did not even catch measles from each other.
> —Violet and Daisy Hilton, from their autobiography

The Hiltons—(no, not Paris and her sister)—were the Jazz Age ideal of showbiz sisters. Pygopagus twins connected at the base of their spines, Daisy and Violet Hilton were raging party girls who worked in vaudeville and Hollywood—at least once they won their emancipation.

Like most conjoined twins, the girls were as different as could be. Daisy loved show business, but Violet always wanted to be a nurse. They shared a common circulatory and nervous system, but were otherwise independent with individual vital parts—including sex organs. They weighed about 160 pounds together, and were reportedly four feet, nine inches tall, although Daisy claimed to be an inch taller than her sister. Actually, they both lied about their heights. "I, Daisy, am blond and green-eyed. I weigh ninety-three

pounds, wear size eleven dresses and one-and-a-half shoe. I am five feet tall," she reveals in their autobiography, while her sister says, "I, Violet, have dark hair and hazel eyes, I've never weighed more than eighty-nine pounds. My shoes are size one. I'm four feet, eleven inches tall."

The sisters certainly had a lot of spunk. Although contemporaries of the nicey-nice Gibb sisters, the Hilton sisters could be considered as the wild children of the conjoined twins world. They were also quite witty and used to playfully say to people whenever they met them for the second or third time: "Maybe you don't remember us." As if anyone could forget them.

Daisy and Violet Hilton were born in Brighton, England, in February 1908. Their natural father was not known; their natural mother, Kate Skinner, was a young unmarried barmaid who could barely take care of herself, let alone a pair of unusual twin girls. She had no idea what to do with her daughters. A midwife named Mary Hilton (who was also Kate's landlady) delivered the babies and she knew exactly what she should do with them. Mary "adopted" (some say bought) the twins from their mother when they were just a few weeks old.

Mary Hilton was not an altruistic woman looking to help out a young girl in trouble, but rather a sadistic tyrant who saw the potential for enormous profit training and touring two young girls. And that was as far as the relationship between Hilton and the young girls ever went. Never for a moment had Violet and Daisy ever thought of this woman as a mother; they were instructed to call her "Auntie" as soon as they could talk. The girls never knew a steady father figure. Auntie had a string of husbands and lovers, all of whom the girls were forced to call "Sir." In addition to being cold and exploitive, Auntie was also terribly abusive. As the girls recalled in their autobiography, "She whipped our backs and shoulders with the buckle end of [a] wide belt."

As soon as the twins could walk, Auntie put them to work. They took singing, dancing, and music lessons, learning to play many instruments including the clarinet, saxophone, piano, and violin. By the time Daisy and Violet were three years old, they were dragged around for a tour of Europe that proved extremely lucrative for Mrs. Hilton.

In 1916, when the girls were eight years old, the "family"—the twins, Auntie, and whichever Sir happened to be sleeping with Auntie at the time—moved from England to San Antonio, Texas. Hence the title "San Antonio's Siamese Twins."

The girls lived a miserable existence. They never saw a penny of their earnings and were forced to live in seclusion when they weren't performing. When the girls were fifteen, Auntie died in Birmingham, Alabama. This would have been a wonderful event except that Mary Hilton willed Daisy and Violet to her grown daughter, Edith Meyers, and Edith's husband—known only as "Sir."

For the next fifteen years, Daisy and Violet lived the same hell they had known with Mary Hilton. But then fate intervened in a kind of backward, lucky way. The twins had signed a publicity photo for a friend, Bill Oliver, which said: "Love Daisy and Violet." They didn't know that Oliver was about to procure a divorce, or that they would be implicated in this divorce, but they were. In 1931, they received notice that they were being sued for $250,000 by Oliver's estranged wife, who was trying to prove the twins were having an affair with Bill because of the word *love* on the signed photos. What seemed like an extremely sticky situation was actually a twist of good luck.

The twins hired attorney Martin J. Arnold to take their case. The girls didn't know that since they were over eighteen years old and of legal age they could be on their own if they chose. They also didn't know they were entitled to all their money. "We've been lonely, rich girls who were really paupers living in practical slavery," they recalled. Arnold was appalled to know that the girls had not seen a penny of the fortune they must have amassed by now, and he helped Violet and Daisy sue Edith Meyers and her husband and finally win their freedom.

The twins were elated. Before this, they had no social interaction and craved all the trappings of the young single life. They always wanted to be "out there" and now, at long last, they finally could be. "We got permanents and pinned up our hair," they wrote in their autobiography. "I, Violet, had always wanted to drink a cocktail. I, Daisy, wanted to smoke a cigarette. And we did."

Unfortunately, their fortune had dwindled to almost nothing, thanks to the avid spending of their guardians. In the late 1920s, the sisters were making about $5,300 a week and saw none of it. Over the course of their careers, they had earned about $2 million; it was nearly all gone. They didn't walk away completely empty-handed, however. In addition to their freedom, they were awarded approximately $100,000: $67,000 in bonds, $12,000 in cash, and $20,000 in personal effects.

Once free, Daisy and Violet could make all their own decisions, and that meant they could act in a movie if they wished. And they did. In 1932, just a year into their new freedom, they starred in *Freaks*, as themselves. In the movie, "Daisy" is married to a stuttering cross-dresser whom "Violet" vehemently dislikes. The running joke in the film is that Violet is the dominant twin of the two, and when the husband barks orders at his wife, Daisy, she doesn't have to obey, as unmarried Violet simply walks their body away from him. They also made another movie in 1950, *Chained for Life*, a quasi-biopic that did poorly. In the film, one of the girls murders her husband for leaving her. A judge decrees that she cannot be incarcerated for the crime because that would mean an innocent woman, namely, the sister, would go to jail.

If love for the Hiltons seemed difficult on celluloid, it can easily be imagined that there was never an ideal romance for either of the Hilton girls. Daisy's first love never panned out. Dan Galvan was a singer in a band who shared her affection and wanted to marry her, but it was too complicated. Violet married James Moore in 1936. Her wedding happened during halftime at the Cotton Bowl as part of the Texas Centennial, in front of about 50,000 people. It was annulled almost immediately.

Daisy married Buddy Sawyer, whose real name was Harold Estep, in 1941. Within ten days he left, without warning, telling the press that "Daisy is a lovely girl. But I guess I'm not the type of fellow that should marry a Siamese twin. . . . In the show business there are times when you get tired of seeing anyone, let alone twin brides."

However unlucky in love the girls were, they were extremely beloved by and popular with everyone who knew them. Reportedly, Frank Lloyd Wright designed a house for them. They were also friendly with Bob Hope, who taught them some dance moves, and Eddie Cantor, with whom they'd sung a number of times. Harry Houdini was also a big fan. It was Houdini, they claim, who taught them how to lead "separate lives" with mind control. He told them, "Live in your minds, girls. It is your only hope for private lives. Just recognize no handicap." As a result, the girls were able to have casual relationships with men, and were also to exist autonomously. One twin could sit up and read in bed while the other slept, and so on.

At the peak of their careers, the girls traveled all over the world and raked in as much as $5,000 a week—even during the Great Depression. Unfortunately, they were horrible with money. It has been said that they could never hold on to it and even they admitted to having "made and lost several fortunes over the course of [their] career."

In 1955, the girls retired from show business. They opened a snack bar in Miami called the Hilton Sisters' Snack Bar, which shortly failed.

In the early 1960s, the girls hopped around, visiting drive-ins to promote the re-release of *Freaks*. Sadly, they were abandoned by their agent on one such jaunt in 1962, in Charlotte, North Carolina. With nowhere to go, they were hired by Charles Reid, who owned a Park-N-Stop grocery store on Wilkinson Boulevard, in Charlotte. He brought them on as a checker-bagger team, and they were eventually promoted to produce weighers.

Throughout their lives, each of the girls had been sick without adverse effect to the other. In 1940, the twins had even been hospitalized because Daisy was stricken with appendicitis. Violet was not ill. She "suffered none of the discomforts of her sister," but she had to undergo the operation just the same.

In 1968, Violet became bedridden with the flu. Daisy wasn't sick at all, and Violet improved. When Daisy then fell ill with the flu, neither recovered. The Hilton sisters had not returned to work in a while and Reid, knowing they had been sick, was worried and called the police. When officers broke into the twins' apartment, the sisters were found dead in their bedroom; it was January 6, 1969.

The Hilton sisters were buried in Forest Lawn Cemetery in Charlotte, strangely sharing a plot with a Vietnam veteran named Troy Thompson. The reason for this was at the time of their deaths,

---

LEGENDARY IMPRESARIO

BOBBY REYNOLDS
(1930–)

Consider Bobby Reynolds a modern-day Barnum—with a playful humbug slant. As he told the *Los Angeles Daily News*, "There's three things that sell—sex, curiosity and thrills. I sell curiosity." And Reynolds, who has been married eleven times, certainly made a name and a good living for himself doing just that.

Reynolds, who refers to himself as "The Greatest Showman in the World," is most famous for exhibiting things that anyone with even the slightest amount of common sense and the smallest grasp of natural history would recognize as fake. Some of his more famous exhibits have included a giant rat (which was really an oversized guinea pig), an "All-Frog Band," and his at-times really atrocious "pickled punks." He also claims to have the real Feejee Mermaid (see page 140) in his possession, though Barnum's famed gaff was believed to have been lost in a fire at the American Museum during the 1860s. But, as it was with Barnum, this is just all part of the fun.

they had no money. A friend of theirs, Troy's mother opted to share her son's funeral plot with them. Even in the end, "sharing" defined the sisters.

Gone but not forgotten, a musical was made of the twins' life in 1997 called *Sideshow*. Although it was a critical success and nominated for several Tony Awards, it folded almost as soon as it opened. To the present day, however, traveling theater companies still play it to great success.

Reynolds had to work from a very early age because his father, a profligate alcoholic, abandoned the family. He worked as a shoeshine boy and as a street peddler to make ends meet. He left school during the third grade, never learning to read or write.

Bobby Reynolds got involved in magic when he was still a kid. By age ten, he was already performing as "The World's Youngest Magician." In the 1940s, he worked at Hubert's Museum and Flea Circus, where he learned the art of being a "talker," as well as how to swallow swords, eat fire, and more. He worked at Coney Island doing magic as well; however, it is his ability as a talker, the guy who stands outside the sideshow tent to bring the spectators in, for which he is legendary.

After working with various circuses in the 1950s and 1960s, Reynolds opened his own show at Coney Island, with a partner, at the end of the 1960s.

Now semi-retired, it's Reynolds's name that most comes up when the new generation of sideshow performers and impresarios talk about their inspiration. As Todd Robbins (see page 181) told the *Los Angeles Times*, "Everything I know about 'talking the front' came from Bobby Reynolds. He's the last of his generation. He's one of the most colorful people I've ever met."

Millie-Christine McKoy

a.k.a. "The Two-Headed Nightingale"
a.k.a. "The Eighth Wonder of the World"
a.k.a. "The United African Twins"
a.k.a. "The Carolina Twins"
(1851–1912)

> I am most wonderfully made. A marvel
> to myself am I.
>
> —Millie-Christine

Of all the conjoined twins featured in this book, Millie-Christine are usually referred to as being one girl. Even the girls that made up Ritta-Christina Parodi (see page 69) were given their own separate identities. But Millie-Christine, although only joined at the coccyx, with their own heads and two normal legs and arms each, liked being considered one person. "Although we speak of ourselves in the plural," they said, "we feel as but *one person*."

Which is not to say they weren't each individual and unique. A physician who examined them when they were nineteen years old said of them: "Millie, though the weaker physically, has the stronger will, and is the dominating spirit, usually controlling their joint movements." He also noted of the girls that "they are usually hungry at the same time, and generally desire the same food and drink."

Unique in pygopagus twins, Millie-Christine shared one set of genitalia. This meant they were examined by doctors more than most conjoined twins. In fact, everywhere they traveled, doctors insisted on taking a peek where they had no business looking. Eventually, when the girls were old and empowered enough, they put a stop to that.

Contemporaries of Chang and Eng, Millie-Christine were born July 11, 1851, in Welches Creek, North Carolina, located in Columbus County. They were delivered by "Aunt Hannah," a slave midwife. Christine emerged first, and Hannah tried to pull the girls apart thinking they were just stuck together with birth fluids. Surprise!

Together they weighed seventeen pounds: Christine twelve, Millie only five. Fully grown, they were barely five feet tall and 170 pounds. Christine was always the stronger one. She was bigger and heavier than her sister, and was even known to pick Millie up by bending over and walking around with Millie on her back. Aside from being connected, the girls were the picture of good health.

Millie-Christine were the children of slaves Monemia, thirty-two years old and mother of seven other children, and Jacob. They had revamped their master's last name, McKay, to McKoy. Their owner, Jabez, a blacksmith, looked into selling Millie-Christine before they were even a year old. John C. Pervis bought the twins in May 1852, with the understanding that one-quarter of what he made exhibiting the twins was to go to McKay. And, if Pervis resold the girls, McKay was to get one-quarter of the sale. Nice guy that he was, McKay allowed Monemia to accompany her daughter(s) while they were with Pervis.

In September 1853, Pervis sold the girls to a man known only as Mr. Brower. Some accounts say they sold for $10,000, some go as high as $30,000, and some as much as $40,000. Brower really couldn't pay, so he brought in Joseph Pearson Smith to back him. Smith, in time, would become as important to the girls as their own kin.

At the end of October that year, the girls hit the road. Everywhere they went, they were near violated by doctors, but who was going to put a stop to it? Their still-enslaved mother? For now, they'd just have to endure it.

When the girls arrived in New Orleans, they were stolen by someone who had tricked Brower into thinking that he was buying them. The crafty buyer had offered Brower $45,000 for the girls, and Brower, apparently not a very good businessman, handed over Millie-Christine the day before he was to receive payment for them.

Smith was enraged—it's hard to say whether it was because of his investment or because he had grown attached to the girls. In any case, he hired a private investigator to find them. The quest was pointless. Once stolen, the girls were only showcased in private venues. It would be some time before the thief got sloppy and the girls would be found.

In August 1854, Millie-Christine were exhibited in Barnum's American Museum. There, they worked with über-famous acts Tom Thumb (see page 13) and Chang and Eng (see page 46); of course, they were much too young to know what was going on. The very next month, Smith found out where they were, but before he could reach them, the girls disappeared again.

Millie-Christine didn't resurface until April 1855, when they turned up in Boston. There, they were purchased from the unscrupulous baby-stealing stranger by a Professor W. J. L. Millar. He brought them to Montreal to exhibit them. Millar either made up an outrageous story about them, or simply repeated what he had been told by the seller. He told spectators during the exhibitions that the girls had been "born in Africa and when only a year old were dragged off together with both their parents, and three brothers and two sisters, and sold into slavery in Cuba."

In July 1855, Millar took his young "performers" overseas. In Liverpool, they were again exhaustively examined. Doctors called them "a natural wonder" (*Liverpool Chronicle*), "little phenomenas" (*Albion*), and "lively and intelligent" (*Liverpool Daily Post*). While in England, Millar hooked up with a man named Thompson, who took on co-ownership of the girls.

Then, and it's not really known why, Millar took the twins and ran out on Thompson. From what later transpired, it can be guessed that Thompson was a shady businessman, and when Millar realized this, he had to dissolve the relationship. Thompson made Millar look like the bad guy and went after him. He published defamatory articles about Millar, and, with the help of the press, Thompson got the twins back and under his own control. He promised the girls they were going home, but this was not true. He, like everyone else, wanted to make some money off the wee oddity; if he had his way, they would probably have been enslaved by him for life.

Luckily, Millar happened to connect with Smith, who, with Monemia, set off for England to rescue the girls. Being faced with the rightful owner, Smith, and the mother, Monemia, Thompson saw his gig was up. He fled but eventually got nabbed and had to plead his case in court. As can be imagined, he was not received well.

When they returned to the States, the girls performed under the surname Smith, which they would continue doing for a while. They still weren't free of Millar, however, who believed he had a contract to manage the girls and was not about to release them from it. Being a very clever man, Smith told Monemia to agree to sign the girls up for another three years. Millar was feeling all cocky that he had won, and he got lazy keeping track of them; Smith smuggled the girls and their mother back to America when Millar wasn't looking. Millar did not come after them again.

Back in the States, Smith became a second father to the girls. His wife gave them lessons in languages, including German, Italian, Spanish, and French, and instructed them in how to conduct themselves like "proper Southern women."

In 1858, the girls exhibited on the Mississippi in the then-popular steamboat tours. [More than likely Millie-Christine were exhibiting on the same tour as Lavinia Warren (see page 19) as this was the same time Lavinia was exhibited on the Mississippi.] For the next few years, Millie-Christine performed in stationary museums. In their act, they were best known for singing. Millie was a contralto and Christine sang soprano. They were known as "The Two-Headed Nightingale," and because they could harmonize nicely, were said to sing beautifully. Over the course of their early years, they had mastered walking together so well that they were even known to dance.

Sadly, Joseph Smith passed away on November 5, 1862, and the girls were devastated. "We were old enough then to mourn the loss of our good master, who seemed to us a father. . . . He was urbane, generous, kind, patient-bearing, and beloved by all," they later wrote. By this time, the girls had become financially successful, and so they took care of Mary Smith, who had been left in dire straits after her husband's death. Moreover, the girls were doing so well, they became the main providers for both the Smiths and the McKoys.

In 1871, following the Civil War, Millie-Christine headed back overseas. They met and became fast friends with Nova Scotia giantess Anna Swan and Martin van Buren Bates (see page 189). In fact, Millie-Christine were even bridesmaids for Anna and Martin's wedding. They remained very close to Anna and Martin until Anna's untimely death. On June 24, 1871, the girls made a special performance for Queen Victoria. She gifted them with a pair of diamond hairpins, which they prized and wore often.

In 1878, Millie-Christine finally returned home, and this time, they were convinced, it was for good. Interestingly enough, the girls brought back the Brothers Magri with them. In just a few years' time, Count Primo Magri would become the second husband of Lavinia Warren.

In 1882, Millie-Christine signed up with a circus for a whopping salary of $25,000. In 1884, after a year off, they once again headed to England. By the late 1880s, the girls decided it was time to retire. They settled in where they started. The girls bought a small farm in Welches Creek, where they had also built homes for their two families. After living their lives on the road, both women were looking forward to staying still for a while. They took great pains in decorating their home themselves and spent as much time as they could entertaining friends and family.

It was a life they had always dreamed of, but alas, it was not destined to last. In 1909, a huge fire in Millie-Christine's home consumed everything. The girls had nothing left. It was all they could do to work up the energy to rebuild their dream home, but it was never quite the same. Unfortunately, the loss took a great toll on them emotionally and they never fully recouped their stamina. Also that year, as if things weren't bad enough, the ever-weak Millie contracted tuberculosis. Millie grew progressively sicker, though Christine was perfectly healthy and seemed completely unaffected by the disease.

Millie passed away three years later, on October 8, 1912; Christine died seventeen hours later, on October 9, praying and singing all the while. The girls were buried at the family home, in a family burial ground still being used. The epitaph on their headstone reads: "A soul with two thoughts. Two hearts that beat as one."

Ritta-Christina Parodi
a.k.a. "l'Enfant Bicephale"
(1829)

> Look at this! Baby born with two heads . . . must be
> from Brooklyn.
>
> —Racetrack from *Newsies* (1992)

Not much documentation exists regarding these twins because they didn't live very long; however, they were not born in Brooklyn. They were the top exhibition in Paris when they lived, despite being only months old, and therefore deserve a mention here as one of the most fascinating sideshow acts of all time.

Ritta-Christina Parodi were born in March 1829, the ninth and tenth children of a thirty-two-year-old Sardinian woman named Maria Teresa Parodi. The girls shared a waist, pelvis, and legs, but had two heads and torsos and two arms each. Their father didn't earn a very good living, at least not one that could comfortably accommodate such a large brood, and the family had no other money. When these connected children were born, therefore, their parents initially saw them as possibly being a terrible burden. The Parodis could see nothing in the future for their daughters but medical bills and grief. Before long, though, they began to recognize the infants as something else: a financial asset.

It occurred to the Parodis that if they exhibited their girls, people just might pay to see them. They were right. The entire family toured Italy and were a sensation. People came for miles to see the baby with two heads. In October 1829, the Parodis headed to Paris, optimistic that more people than ever before would come to see Ritta-Christina, and that they had found their ticket to the "good life."

They were certainly right about the public. The Parisians could not get enough of what they called *"l'enfant bicephale"* (the child with two heads). The authorities, however, were not crazy about the act. It may be more accurate to say that they were disgusted, appalled, *degoute.* They looked for everything they could to shut

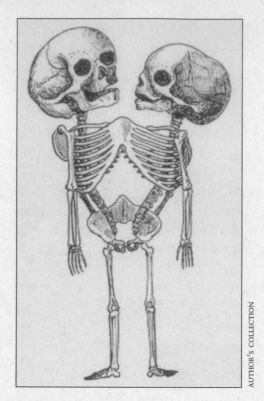

AUTHOR'S COLLECTION

down the show, and when the girls' health began to deteriorate, they finally had reason.

The right twin, Ritta, had always been weaker than her left twin sister, Christina, and now she had developed the illness that would kill them both. The Parodis were not yet making enough money to heat the tiny apartment where they lived with all their children. Even though it wasn't the dead of winter, it was still cold enough to affect a baby. Ritta developed acute bronchitis, which, interestingly enough, seemed to have no effect on Christina.

Eight months and eleven days after breathing their first breaths, Ritta's little lungs couldn't take anymore. She died on November 23, 1829, followed instantly by Christina, who had still not exhibited any sign of the illness. The authorities blamed the twins' death on parental neglect and abuse. They claimed that the Parodis overworked their infant daughters and did not feed or otherwise care for them properly.

The parents were in a whole heap of trouble until the body of the girls was taken to be autopsied. Upon careful examination, doctors learned that the girls probably weren't going to live very long anyway. Although Christina was essentially healthy, Ritta had a severely malformed heart. Because they shared a circulatory system, it was only a matter of time that they could survive. The bronchitis made it quicker. They shared a large and small intestine and a set of genitalia, but each had her own uterus. Additionally, they each had their own stomach, spleen, and pancreas.

Unfortunately, no photos were ever taken of the twins. The skeleton sketch on page 70 is the only existing image of the Parodi twins.

Giovanni and Giacomo Tocci

a.ka. "The Two-Headed Boy"
a.k.a. "The Blended Tocci Brothers"
a.k.a. "The Greatest Wonder of Nature"

(1877–1940)

> Originally the story was called "Those Extraordinary Twins." I meant to make it very short. I had seen a picture of a youthful Italian "freak" or "freaks" which was—or which were—on exhibition in our cities—a combination consisting of two heads and four arms joined to a single body and a single pair of legs—and I thought I would write an extravagantly fantastic little story with this freak of nature for hero—or heroes.
>
> —Mark Twain, explaining his inspiration, the Tocci Brothers, in the preface of his novel, *Those Extraordinary Twins*

As noted previously, even conjoined twins are never truly identical, and that especially pertains to their personalities. For the famed Tocci brothers, this could not be more true. Giacomo Tocci, the brother on the left, was intellectually slow and reputed to be

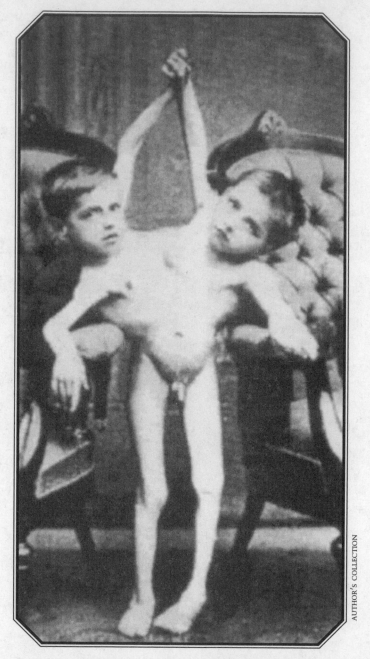

AUTHOR'S COLLECTION

Giovanni and Giacomo Tocci

dull. His counterpart, Giovanni Tocci, was said to be lively, intelligent, and quick witted. In addition, when one was sick, the other was well; when one slept, the other was typically awake. And that's the way it was with "the famous two-headed boy."

On October 4, 1877, a nineteen-year-old woman gave birth to twin sons in Locana, Italy. It was quite startling to the young mother to discover that her sons were connected to each other. They had two heads, two torsos, and two arms each. Later findings would reveal that they each had their own heart, lungs, stomachs, and distinct respiratory and circulatory systems. But from the sixth rib down, they were one boy, sharing an anus, a penis, and two legs.

To say the father was in shock over the birth would be a gross understatement. Instead of celebrating the arrival of his two otherwise healthy sons, he suffered a complete nervous breakdown. His mental collapse led to his being institutionalized. And despite how robust the boys were, doctors were sure they wouldn't survive.

Following the father's recovery, about a month after the birth, he began seeing his boys in a different light. The boys need not be a financial burden at all; they could be the Toccis' ticket to incredible wealth. He took his one-month-old sons to the Royal Academy of Medicine in Turin to let doctors examine them and validate their strange condition.

When the boys were four months old, the Tocci boys' father cashed in his golden ticket, appointing himself the boys' manager and, along with his young wife, toured them all over Europe. At first, they had no special talent; what could any four-month-old child be expected to do? They were simply an attraction for gawkers.

As they grew, they adjusted to their unusual body, but one thing they never quite mastered was walking. Each brother had control of the leg on his side of the body, thus they never truly coordinated themselves to walking properly. Moreover, Giacomo had a clubfoot. Instead of walking upright, therefore, they crawled on the ground together like a spider. Standing was also difficult. In pictures, they are usually positioned with their arms in the air, hands joined.

When they were old enough, each brother learned to write—one with left hand, one with right—and each reportedly spoke three languages. The brothers were also thought to be artistic, though most sources claim Giovanni was more talented than Giacomo.

The Tocci twins and their manager parents arrived in the United States in 1891 where they hooked up with various shows; they traveled around for the next six years, but eventually burned out.

By their twenties, they had had enough. For one, the twins had never liked the showbiz lifestyle. If their father hadn't been so controlling, they never would have agreed to his plans. Once they came of legal age, however, they no longer had to obey their father. The brothers were now entitled to their earnings, which were quite substantial; at the peak of their popularity, the Tocci twins were pulling in a whopping thousand bucks a week.

What happened to Giacomo and Giovanni after they retired differs from account to account. Most sources agree that the boys left the United States and returned to their native Italy, where they lived in relative seclusion in a small town near Venice for the remainder of their days. Most accounts also agree that just after their retirement, the boys married women who were sisters. (Apparently not uncommon for conjoined male twins because Chang and Eng—see page 46—and Lucio and Simplicio Godina, also wedded sisters.) The marriages created a small hiccup of a scandal, and reportedly resulted in children. But the scandal never escalated to "uproar."

How the Tocci brothers died—Who died first? How long before the other followed? What was the cause of death?—is not known. Most sources do concur, however, that the "extraordinary twins" perished sometime in 1940.

Armless and Legless Wonders

Eli Bowen and Charles Tripp

Eli Bowen
a.k.a. "The Legless Acrobat"
a.k.a. "The Handsomest Man in Showbiz"
a.k.a. "Wonder of the Wide, Wide World!"
(1844–?)

> My family never seemed embarrassed by him.
> We were all impressed by him. He was a very
> successful man. I wish I knew more about him.
> —Gabrielle Bowen, great-granddaughter of Eli Bowen, as featured
> on James Mundie's "Prodigies" collection (missioncreep.com)

Charles B. Tripp
a.k.a. "The Armless Photographer"
(1855–1939)

> He was a real hero in every sense of the word and
> overcame odds in life that would have submerged
> many a man with less determination and spirit.
> —From an obituary of Charles B. Tripp

li Bowen is widely remembered for many things—his candor, his uncanny good looks, his effect on women. His most amazing talent, however, was his astonishing acrobatic skill. As part of his routine, he performed cartwheels, somersaults, and backflips, which may be impressive for any circus acrobat, but Eli Bowen accomplished these feats with phocomelia, a condition that causes "seal limbs." Essentially, he had arms but no legs. Eli had no "feet," per se, but he did have what were more like "flippers," which sprouted from his hips; he used these to help propel himself into his stunts.

Born in Ohio in 1844, Eli was one of ten children. Neither his parents nor his siblings shared his condition; they were all normal. Regardless, he was well accepted in his family, who always showed support and love.

As a toddler, Eli, like most children his age, was desperate to get around by himself. Without legs, though, he wasn't going to do this by walking. After much struggling, he figured out how to move himself. It wasn't easy for Bowen to learn how to use his body, but once he did, he used it to great effect. He had learned to walk on his hands using wooden blocks so that his hips would not drag on the ground, because his arms, when he was small, were not much longer than his torso. As a result of learning to walk on his hands, he developed tremendous upper-body strength, like Johnny Eck (see page 78). As he grew older, Eli learned to parlay that strength into a series of acrobatic stunts he would experiment with and perfect. By the time he was thirteen years old, he decided to go public with what he could do. He joined Major Brown's Coliseum, a traveling show, in 1857.

In 1870, Bowen teamed up with P. T. Barnum and toured the world. His act consisted of a series of somersaults, backflips, and jokes thrown in for good measure. Eli Bowen's most famous stunt was done in collaboration with the armless Canadian, Charles Tripp (see page 77).

Bowen and Tripp posed on a tandem bicycle. Tripp "pedaled" while Bowen "steered," and, both typically good-natured chaps, they joked the whole time. Tripp would chide his legless friend to "Watch your step." Bowen would retort: "Keep your hands off me." Both working with Barnum at the time, they made it into a hugely successful skit and are generally remembered as a team because of it.

Later that year, Eli Bowen fell in love with a knockout named Mattie Haines, and she bowled him over. She was quite strikingly normal, and by normal, ordinary is not implied. Apparently Miss Haines was something of a "hot commodity" and never sat home on a Saturday night. But there was something about Eli that was unlike anyone she had ever known before. She also fell desperately in love with him and in a few short months, the two were married. The Bowens enjoyed many happy years together, and they had four normal boys: Frank, Robert, Adrian, and Victor.

In the mid-1880s, Eli Bowen got his fill of show business—excitement-wise and financially—and he decided it was time to retire. He moved his family to Ogden, California, where he lived out his life. Unfortunately, there is no known record of his death.

Think of Charles Tripp as an oddball among oddities. The Canadian-born performer always wore a business suit, on and off stage, and was always cracking people up. Not much is known about Tripp's early years at all, except that he was born in Woodstock, Canada, in 1855. When he was eighteen years old, he crossed the border into the United States to work with Barnum, who was very impressed by all the things Tripp could do without arms. Using his feet and toes, Tripp could write and take pictures. He could also dress himself and shave, and he was an accomplished woodworker. Tripp traveled many years with Barnum.

During the time he was with Barnum, he met another fellow, a few years older, who was also working with Barnum. Tripp clicked instantly with Eli Bowen (see page 76), and together with "The Legless Acrobat," he created the aforementioned bicycle stunt, one of the funniest sight gags of the time.

When Barnum died, Tripp continued to work in sideshows, first with Ringling Bros. and Barnum & Bailey Circus, who billed him as "the armless photographer," and then with several other traveling shows. He toured for more than fifty years.

Tripp reportedly married late in life, but as it was part of his shtick to be an eligible bachelor, he is never pictured with his wife. Charles Tripp died in Salisbury, North Carolina, in 1939.

Johnny Eck

a.k.a. "John Eckhardt"
a.k.a. "The Only Living Half Boy"
a.k.a. "Nature's Greatest Mistake"
a.k.a. "The Boy Wonder"

(1911–1991)

> I met hundreds and thousands of people, and none
> finer than the midgets and the Siamese twins and
> the caterpillar man and the bearded woman and the
> human seal with little flippers for hands. I never
> asked them any embarrassing questions and they
> never asked me, and God, it was a great adventure.
>
> —Johnny Eck, on his experience with other sideshow freaks

Like many of the acts featured in this book, Johnny Eck had a broad range of interests and talents outside of his sideshow life. Physically a "half man," Eck was a consummate gentleman. He always dressed in formalwear and he was all class. He never let his condition affect him, that is, not until quite late in his life. So confident in who he was, Eck had been known to say: "If I want to see freaks, I can just look out the window."

In addition to being a performer and an actor, Johnny Eck was a gifted painter, an artist, a musician, and a gymnast. Believe it or not, he loved auto racing and even raced his own car. In 1938, he climbed to the top of the Washington Monument on his hands. He was an enthusiastic storyteller, and, for most of his life, he was good tempered and charming, and displayed a gusto for living. Sadly for Eck, as time went on, he lost most of his patience with the world. At the time of his death at age eighty, with the world changing drastically every day, he was ready to go.

Still and all, Eck continues to be a source of great curiosity. In 2001, for instance, Leonardo DiCaprio had signed on to a film project to play both Johnny and his twin brother, Robert, in a movie based on the sideshow sensation's life. Although slated for release in late 2003 or early 2004, at the time of this writing several issues have held up production. It is not known when or if the film will hit theaters.

On August 27, 1911, a second boy was born to John Eckhardt and Amelia Dippel Eckhardt, twenty minutes after his twin brother Robert. As Eck himself would later relate, the younger twin, John, looked as though he was "snapped off at the waist." Reportedly, everyone who witnessed the birth was terrified, though John's twin, Robert, was born perfectly normal.

Johnny measured 18 inches long, which is pretty tall considering he had no legs. Because a normal baby measures between 19 and 21 inches long, it's more likely that Johnny measured between 10 and 13 inches long. Fully grown, he reached 28 inches and 37 pounds. Over the course of his life, he supposedly never weighed more than 60 pounds.

Johnny and Robert grew up in Baltimore, at 622 North Milton Avenue, the house they both died in. Today, it's not considered a great neighborhood, but it was a decent place to raise a family in the early twentieth century.

From early on, Amelia Eckhardt put Robert in charge of Johnny. An older sister, who was between eight and twelve when they were born, named Caroline (or Carolyn—shows up both ways), was never as close to the boys as they were with each other. Surely, it wouldn't be a stretch to say that the twins were inseparable throughout their lives. The only times they spent apart were when Robert joined the Navy during World War II and when Johnny was in Hollywood working on various film projects.

The relationship between the brothers is what Johnny prized the most, and most people who knew them thought the same. Clearly, the main focus of the DiCaprio movie mentioned earlier is the connection between the two brothers, and Eck's career, which was nurtured by this bond.

Though Johnny Eck may have possessed only half a body, he had a full-fledged desire to live his life to the fullest, even from an early age. At only one year old, Johnny learned to "walk" on his hands. As a result of Eck's ability to move himself around, he had an incredibly well-developed upper body, which helped him perform amazing acrobatics later in his career, just like Eli Bowen (see page 76) before him.

In addition to being physically strong, both brothers were highly intelligent and adept. Both could read and write by the time they were four years old. So sharp was Johnny Eck, in fact, that it has been alleged by several sources that he probably possessed a genius-level IQ. Besides his swift intelligence, as a kid, Johnny was very religious and loved to preach in his living room. As another one of his many aspirations, he dreamed of becoming a minister. (As a side note to this, his parents didn't maintain very high aspirations for him. They encouraged him to become a typist.)

School was not a huge challenge for Eck. He easily mastered his studies and excelled in his classes; he was also a very popular kid. Instead of his lack of legs being a cause of fear or scorn to the other kids, Johnny was wholeheartedly embraced by his classmates. Many even went out of their way to help him when he needed it. Even though his career would start up while he was still in school, he finished his education and graduated from a Baltimore college.

In 1924, Johnny and Robert attended a carnival that had come to Baltimore. There, they were spectators to a magic show, which would open up many new doors for the brothers. The magician, John McAslan, spotted Johnny in the audience and pursued him. McAslan eventually talked Johnny into retaining him as manager and brought Eck into the sideshow. Johnny had one condition: McAslan must provide a job for Robert.

Johnny Eck took to the circus like a fish to water. He developed an animal training act, performed dazzling feats of acrobatics and strength, and amazed people with his stunts on the trapeze. Because he had had musical training, Johnny was also known to do numbers from time to time. "I was a performer, walked a tight rope, worked on trapeze, juggled," said Eck, "I did everything."

Johnny Eck loved the sideshow world. He adored everything about it. "God how I loved to get out under those big tents," he said in his autobiography. "I loved the animals, and I loved camping out." But more than any of that, he lived to perform. He relished the attention. He remembered how he was advertised and it just elated him:

"The banners we had out front . . . [McAslan] got me the biggest one he could. They were ten feet high and twenty feet long, and colored."

In addition to his work in the sideshow, Eck spent some time in the 1930s as a display in one of Robert Ripley's odditoriums. In addition to his work as a "freak," Eck and his brother had their own dance band called the Red Phantom Dance Band. On the off-season, Johnny and Robert spent their time composing for and conducting this twelve-piece orchestra in Baltimore in the 1920s and 1930s.

In 1932, Johnny Eck got his chance to act on the big screen in director Tod Browning's *Freaks*. Like most of the actors in the film, Eck would essentially play himself. Of course, Eck's character had something of a sinister bent. He was a cordial fellow in the beginning of the movie; however, by the time the freaks decided that Cleo was up to no good, most of Eck's screen time was spent suspiciously peering into windows, softly whispering, and menacingly polishing his gun to torment the evil trapeze tart who was trying to murder his friend. (Later in life, Eck had a large collection of guns, but is reported to have loved that gun, which was not a prop but an actual firearm from his collection, more than any other.)

Eck had mixed feelings about his co-stars. Sometimes he would go out of his way to be "one of them"; other times, he avoided them, calling them "a happy, noisy crowd. And I was bent on being sophisticated. . . . I really didn't relate with that crowd of freaks. I just couldn't mix with them. They were childish, silly, and in a world all their own."

Freaks would not be Johnny's only film. In the 1930s and early 1940s, he played a "bird creature" in a few of Hollywood's onslaught of *Tarzan* films at that time, which starred Johnny Weissmuller as "Tarzan" and Maureen O'Sullivan as "Jane." Unbilled, Johnny Eck appeared in *Tarzan the Ape Man* (1932). He was credited as a "Gooney-Bird" in *Tarzan Escapes* (1936), and then he appeared, unbilled again, in *Tarzan's Secret Treasure* (1941).

After making the last *Tarzan* film, Eck grew weary of show business and decided to retire. To make a living, he and Robert decided to open a penny arcade. Unfortunately, this business venture failed after only a few years.

Eck had always wanted to be a train engineer, among his 342 other career aspirations, that is. So, in the 1950s, he and Robert bought a miniature train ride and operated it in a local park to give rides to youngsters. Eck adored children and was always good to them, and for the most part, when they became accustomed to looking at him, they were not frightened of Johnny Eck. He had a wonderful warmth and way with kids. Even into his old age, Eck would perform puppet shows on the front stoop of the house he shared with Robert.

Johnny Eck slipped into oblivion once he retired from show business. He made a quiet living as a successful screen painter, actually painting pictures on screen doors as a way to give home owners privacy.

When *Freaks* was released on video in the mid-1980s, and a whole new generation of people had seen the film, it was the beginning of the end for Eck. The film brought *Freaks* fanatics to his house in droves. Teenagers especially would drop in on him at any time—ironic for a man who was now making his living providing privacy for others.

In the last years of his life, Johnny began writing his autobiography. A friend encouraged this as a good way for Johnny to supplement his now-meager living, so he bought a typewriter and set himself to the task. Though he never finished it—in fact, he barely started it—nor did he ever have a publisher for it, he reportedly had called R. Crumb to paint his portrait for the book's cover. Crumb was delighted, but Eck had a change of heart after he viewed the painting Crumb made for him. He thought it was too cartoonish and that people who saw it would not take him seriously.

In the last few years of his life, Eck became very bitter and even more than a little racist. Besides being hounded constantly by new fans, he was in a heated battle with his next-door neighbor, a black man known only as Gaffer. Apparently, Eck had resorted to some pretty outrageous methods to rid himself of his detested neighbor—including voodoo.

A robbery at Johnny's home on January 18, 1987, proved to be the straw that broke the camel's back. Eck, now in his mid-seventies, was still strong and robust, but not like when he was younger. The humiliation of one of the robbers sitting on him and immobilizing him, while he was ridiculed and ripped off, was enough for him to be put off life for good. He became a recluse for his remaining days.

Johnny Eck died of a heart attack on January 5, 1991. He was seventy-nine years old. He is buried in the family plot at Greenmount Cemetery, in Baltimore, where he shares a headstone with Robert, who died about four years later.

Otis Jordan
a.k.a. "The Human Cigarette Factory"
a.k.a. "The Frog Boy"
(1926–1990)

> I don't understand it. How can she say I'm being taken advantage of? Hell, what does she want for me—to be on welfare?
>
> —Otis Jordan, after a "do-gooder" took legal action
> to prevent him from being exhibited

Otis Jordan was the last of the natural-born sideshow "freaks" ever able to exhibit themselves for money. When Otis came into the sideshow, not only had the backlash begun, it had gotten rampant. But Otis was a fighter. He was a highly religious man who believed God put him on this earth for a purpose, and if that purpose was to perform, then he had no choice but to defend his right to work. "I have a deep faith in God and this has seen me through many hard times," he said. "I say 'Never give up.' And I never have."

Jordan was born in Barnesville, Georgia, to a loving but poor family of six brothers and sisters, all normal. Although Jordan had limbs, they were useless to him. They were ossified, meaning they were essentially paralyzed; his limbs were also very short. He could use only the thumb and index finger of his right hand.

His intellect was above average, and Otis was determined to attend school. At first, he had to rely on one of his brothers to carry

Otis Jordan

him. Soon, that stopped being comfortable for him. In addition to being highly intelligent, Otis also possessed a fiercely independent spirit, and it wasn't long before he felt the frustration of not being able to get along by himself. Thus he made up his mind to do something about it. The end product as much as the process exemplified the kind of patience and determination that generally saw Otis through his difficult life.

After carefully reasoning what it would entail, Otis devised a kind of "carriage" for himself, as he later detailed for Johnny Meah. Otis had a wagon that friends and family transported him in, and he figured out the logistics of getting a couple of the family's goats to do the pulling. He strapped the goats to the wagon; then, he created a harness with rope and a broom handle. In a month, he had it down pat and working. "My daddy laughed and laughed—and then he cried and hugged me," Otis told Meah about his invention. "Next day he fixed up a real little harness and board with an old pillow that I could sit on." In time, Otis completed his schooling and even earned a mail-order degree.

When fully grown, Otis was about the size of an average four-year-old. His head and face, however, grew and matured as Otis did—along with his intellect. Eventually, Otis learned to drive a car with special controls, though it can't be confirmed whether or not he actually obtained a driver's license.

Even though he had no use of arms, legs, fingers—except the two—and toes, he boasted an ability to create certain crafts and to repair small appliances. But he couldn't make a living doing these. Nor could he properly support himself selling pencils or newspapers, ventures he tried out but that were short-lived. He didn't know what he was going to be able to do to support himself and it was a cause of great frustration to him.

One night, when the carnival was in town, Otis Jordan headed out with some friends to check out the action. A friend pulled Otis along in his wagon, and Otis begged him to stop at the hootchy-kootchy tent, which was right next to the freak tent.

Because of his devotion to Otis, the freak tent made the friend uncomfortable; Otis, however, was intrigued. At last, he saw an opportunity to stop living off his friends and family, to become really independent. "It was impossible for me to get a job until 1963 when a carnival played in my home town," he later recalled.

When Otis met Dick Burnett that night, the showman was instantly impressed with the little shriveled up man. But when he found out Otis also had a trick, Burnett was sold. You see, Otis had been practicing and had perfected one of Prince Randian's (see page

87) old tricks. "I had learned to roll and light a cigarette with my lips and mouth," he said, "and demonstrated this to the sideshow manager. I was hired on the spot and have been in this business ever since."

Otis began performing with Burnett that spring. Now he had a job, an income, and a sense of purpose. No longer an "invalid" who relied on his friends and family to "carry" him through life, he was now making enough money to support himself. He was billed as "the Frog Boy," and throughout the course of his career, he worked with several showmen, including Ward Hall and Johnny Meah.

Otis performed with pride in his work and had a sense of dignity about what he was doing. At first, his performances consisted of him just sitting there, rolling his cigarettes and allowing people to gawk at him. He was absolutely terrified to speak, though he was encouraged to often. One night, he finally got up his courage, and, from that point on, Otis added lecturing to his performance.

Amiable Otis had many friends, which proved essential for him, especially during the off-season. An unfortunate reality of his life was that he needed constant care, and for this, he had to rely on friends. Among his strongest allies was his manager, promoter, and caretaker, John Bradshaw. Otis lived with Bradshaw and his family in an apartment at Coney Island, which was a great deal better than living in an institution, where he may have ended up had he not had a job.

Soon, a good thing for Otis would come to an end. Otis was working with Sutton's Sideshow, still as "the Frog Boy," when a "do-gooder" was offended by his act. She was appalled that such a poor specimen of humanity should be showing himself for money at the New York State Fair. Because of her indignant outrage and actions taken, Otis was out of work for the season. This meant lost revenue, and he had to go to court to fight for his right to perform. The legal fees alone were almost enough reason to throw in the towel, but giving up was not Otis Jordan's style.

As Melvin Burkhart remembered the ordeal: "At one time we had a little man, called Otis Jordan, that could roll up cigarettes with his lips and light it, you know, and he had little skinny arms and he had legs that were all screwed up, you know, scrooched up like that. He couldn't move them or couldn't walk on them or anything but he did a hell of an act and he was excluded from our show. He couldn't work at all because the do-gooders had said he was being exploited. . . . He didn't have any place to go. You know, he couldn't understand it. Why the hell are they doing this to me?"

In 1987, Otis won his right to go back to work, this time at Coney Island. But, because of the time frame in which he came into the business, he had to change his name. It was no longer politically correct to refer to a human being as a "Frog Boy." "The Human Cigarette Factory" (which, had he lived ten years longer would have been changed as well, no doubt) worked nearly up till the day he died.

Otis passed away from kidney failure while visiting family in Georgia in 1990.

Prince Randian

a.k.a. "The Human Caterpillar"
a.k.a. "The Living Torso"
a.k.a. "The Human Worm"
a.k.a. "The Pillow Man"
a.k.a. "The Sausage Man"
(1871–1934)

> The love of beauty is a deep seated urge which dates
> back to the beginning of civilization. The revulsion
> with which we view the abnormal, the malformed and
> the mutilated is the result of long conditioning by our
> forefathers.
>
> —from the prologue to *Freaks*

There is not much information available on this unusual enigma of a performer, but anyone who had ever seen him in action would not doubt his inclusion among the most fascinating of sideshow acts. He was, in a word, a marvel.

Prince Randian (a stage name, though his real name is not known), was born in British Guyana, South America, in 1871. He was brought to the United States in 1889 by a scout for Barnum. Barnum touted him as "the Human Caterpillar." Randian toured the United States and Europe with Barnum's "Greatest Show on Earth" for years, even after Barnum was gone. He also toured with other shows, as well as exhibited himself at Coney Island.

Prince Randian was Hindu, and he spoke several languages,

LEGENDARY IMPRESARIO

Samuel W. Gumpertz
(1868–1935?)

If it were not for the efforts of Samuel W. Gumpertz, Coney Island would never have become the legendary land of wonder it has been for more than a hundred years. He brought the dreams, his dreams, into Dreamland, creating a magical place of fantasy and fun, which all began with the introduction of freaks.

Samuel was born into a fairly normal family in 1868; the problem was, he wasn't your everyday average guy. He didn't quite fit in with his relatives, and, at the age of nine, he ran away from home to join a clan that really understood him: the circus. Starting out at the Montgomery and Queens Circus, Gumpertz trained himself to do various acrobatic feats, including walking on his hands.

Gumpertz wasn't at all the type to settle in to one thing for too long. Soon enough, he got "itchy" and had to move around. Among the other jobs he held were performing kids' parts at the Tivoli Opera House in San Francisco and working as a rancher in Texas. At age twelve, he joined Buffalo Bill's Wild West Show, and, in his late twenties and early thirties, he began producing plays and even opened a string of theaters.

learned from his travels. Besides Hindi, he was fluent in English, German, and French. The multi-talented torso claimed that, for the most part, he controlled what he had of a "body" with his mind. He willed himself to use his mouth to do things.

Randian could write, paint, and shave with his mouth (that last one had to have been quite a thing to see; shaving was up close and personal). And in those days, there was no alternative to a straight razor, so it's a feat in itself that his face was never covered in bloody

In 1904, Gumpertz came to Coney Island's Dreamland, where he changed the landscape of the seaside town forever. He developed a town in miniature called "Lilliputia," also known as "Midget City." When it was completed, 300 little people moved in. Among the famous residents of this tiny community were Lavinia Warren (see page 19) and her second husband, Count Magri. The city in miniature boasted its own government complete with police and fire department. It was designed to give the little people a venue for exhibition as well as a place to live.

In 1905, Gumpertz brought in a tribe of more than 200 Bantocs and created a new colony for them at Coney Island. In 1908, he was appointed general manager. Now with the power to do everything he wanted in the park, he took his passions, human oddities and circus performers, and delivered them to the public. Gumpertz traveled around the world extensively to collect new "spectacles."

In 1911, Dreamland burned down, and Gumpertz rebuilt with a new game plan. From that point on, he devoted his time to exhibiting freaks, who included Lionel, the Lion-Faced Man (see page 138); Eli Bowen (see page 76); and Zip, the What Is It? (see page 121).

In 1929, Gumpertz left Coney Island to run the Barnum & Bailey Circus. He died a few years later, though the exact date cannot be found.

gashes or scars. Reportedly, Randian also built the box in which he stored his smoking paraphernalia (yes, also with his mouth).

His most famous trick, and one copied later by Otis "the Frog Boy" Jordan (see page 83), was to roll, light, and smoke a cigarette, using only his mouth. He dazzled sideshow audiences with this one every performance, and then brought it to the big screen when he played a role in *Freaks*.

How he got into the film is not known. However, seeing him in it, another one of Randian's talents shone through: Prince Randian could also act, as anyone who's seen *Freaks* can attest to. His one line was essentially incoherent, but his facial expressions and gestures spoke volumes. When he wiggles through the mud close to the end, knife in his mouth, menacing as hell, it's quite possibly the most frightening aspect of that terrifying scene.

But that was purely an act. In real life, Randian was a decent, loving man. He eventually got married to another performer, known only as "Princess Sarah," and the happy couple brought several children into the world. The Prince Randians lived in Patterson, New Jersey, so he could be close to Coney Island and other venues where he exhibited himself.

Randian's final public appearance was at Sam Wagner's Fourteenth Street Museum, on December 19, 1934. He died later that month, cause unknown, at the age of fifty-three.

Ann E. Leak Thompson
a.k.a. "The Armless Lady"
a.k.a. "The Armless Wonder"
(1839–?)

> Miss Leak . . . feels no little delicacy at seeking, to make the deprivation which she suffers in the entire absence of arms at her birth, the occasion of gain to her, by gratifying the eye, oftentimes, of a curious public; though adverse to it at first, and till circumstances, changing, necessitated such a course.

AUTHOR'S COLLECTION

Ann E. Leak

She can, in this way . . . best meet the obligations
which she owes to herself and her aged parents.
— Ann E. Leak, explaining why it was okay
    for such a proper lady to be paid to have
    the public gawk at her

s this description, written by Ann Leak, demonstrates, Ann was not exactly what you'd call the "show business type." Clearly, she was determined to emphasize the dignity in what she was doing. She was not a flashy, outgoing sort; she was the epitome of a proper Victorian lady.

Ann E. Leak was pious and pristine; she was dainty and demure. In many ways, she was a matron well ahead of her marriage. She donned very plain clothes and always wore a somber expression. But she had another side.

You couldn't really call it a dark side—but perhaps more of a dark streak. She had a wicked sense of humor when it came to her condition, which usually came out when she signed cartes de visites for fans. Here are just a few to get a taste:

> Hands deprived
> Toes derived.
>
> So you perceive, it's really true,
> When hands are lacking, toes will do.
>
> I write poetry and prose
> Holding my pen between my toes!

This quick wit, partnered with her incredible abilities, made Ann a hugely popular attraction. Aside from whipping out sharp Dorothy Parker–esque rhymes, Leak was adept at many different things. She was usually pictured on her cartes de visite with crocheting and embroidery, and these were not props. During her performances, Ann would demonstrate her mastery of these, two of her favorite hobbies, with her feet.

Ann's other passion came out in her work. Onto her crafts, she usually embroidered phrases like "Holiness in the Lord," while on her cards she stuck to the more madcap messages like the ones given in the previous examples, a clear indication that she could play her role and play along with what the sideshow expected of her, and she could laugh at herself.

Ann Leak was born in Georgia on December 23, 1839. Like many Victorian oddities, she believed that her condition was caused by maternal impression. The story goes that her father was a raging and abusive alcoholic. As Ann related the tale, one night he came home utterly intoxicated: "He had his overcoat thrown over his shoulders without his arms in his sleeves," she said. When her pregnant mother saw him drunk and angry again like this, the stress was too much for her to bear, and the image transferred to her fetus. As a result, Ann was born without arms.

When she was in her forties, Ann married William R. Thompson. One child, a boy, is typically featured in photos of Ann and her husband. Because Ann had married relatively late in her life, it's impossible to know if this boy is a son or a stepson; if he were her natural-born child, he would have been born when she was well into her forties, very uncommon at that time.

MORE TO LOVE

Myrtle Corbin
a.k.a. "Josephene Myrtle Corbin"
a.k.a. "The Four-Legged Woman"
(1868–1927)

> The duplication in this case begins just above the waist, the spinal column dividing at the third lumbar vertebra, below this point everything being double.... [A doctor who examined Myrtle Corbin] ... said [Myrtle] utilized her outside legs for walking; he also remarks that when he informed her that she was pregnant on the left side she replied, "I think you are mistaken; if it had been on my right side I would come nearer believing it. ..." After further questioning he found, from the patient's observation, that her right genitals were almost invariably used for coitus.
>
> —From a description of Myrtle Corbin
> from *Anomalies and Curiosities of Medicine*

For the most part with parasitic twins, the one who is the "parasite" typically has no defining characteristics at all. It's simply part of a body, hanging off the other twin, growing from its dominant sibling. In the case of Myrtle Corbin, however, the parasitic twin

AUTHOR'S COLLECTION

Myrtle Corbin

did more than just hang there; "she" conceived and birthed some of Myrtle's children.

Josephene Myrtle Corbin was born in Lincoln County, Tennessee, in 1868, though some accounts stipulate that she was actually a Texas girl. In any case, Myrtle was a dipygus, meaning "double buttocks," twin. She had a set of legs growing between her own legs, and in between those legs was a vagina that led to a fully functioning female reproductive system.

Nothing is really known about her early life—not until she began exhibiting herself in 1881. She was very popular and more than a few sideshow spectators were curious about how she "used" the other twin. She also had the medical community's rapt attention. Everywhere she went doctors were falling all over themselves to examine her.

When Myrtle was nineteen years old, she took a fascination of her own with the medical community—or at least one member of it: She married Dr. Clinton Bicknell. Myrtle left the exhibition life behind to enjoy being a doctor's wife. She and Dr. Bicknell had five healthy and perfectly normal children. Myrtle gave birth to four girls and a boy. Reportedly, three of these children were born from one body and two from the other.

Once Myrtle left the business, she inspired others to fake her special attribute, but all proved to be frauds. In fact, there's only ever been one case of dipygus twins giving birth, and that was Myrtle and her "sister."

Laloo and Piramal Sami

Laloo
a.k.a. "The Four-Legged, Four-Armed Man"
(1874-1905)

Piramal Sami
a.k.a. "The Hindoo [*sic*] Wonder"
(1888–?)

> More incredible than the man with two bodies—
> a mixture of brother and sister!
>
> —From a pamphlet hyping Laloo

aloo, who is not recorded anywhere as having had any other name, had all the makings of a celebrity. The handsome boy, who hailed from India, was exotic and suave. He dressed extravagantly, lived every minute of his life to the fullest, and went out in a blaze while he was still young and before his image could sour. Consider him the Valentino of the freaks—that is, Valentino with a twin "sister" sprouting from his midsection.

Not much is known about Laloo's life before he signed up with the sideshow, except that he was born in 1874, in Oovin, Oudh, India, the second—and third—of four children. His family was Muslim, and this is a tradition he took with him on his extensive travels throughout the world.

Like so many sideshow performers, Laloo earned terrific amounts of money exhibiting himself. His act was very basic; essentially all he did was come on stage dressed impeccably, holding his twin's arms outstretched. No matter how much money he earned, however, he never seemed to have any. Apparently, Laloo was an incurable spendthrift who accumulated nothing.

Like Piramal Sami (see page 99), Laloo was exhibited as being a male with a female twin. This was actually pure humbug. While the twin was typically dressed in feminine attire, the twin was undeniably

Laloo in "performance" mode.

male with a perfectly formed penis. Maybe it was too obscene in Victorian times for a handsome man to walk around with two penises, but perhaps more likely, it was more sensational for the body of a woman to be growing out of a man.

Laloo's twin's torso, arms, and legs grew out of the front of his own torso; there was no head. Laloo's nervous system was connected to the twin's, so when someone touched the twin, Laloo could feel it. They also shared a circulatory system. Aside from a jerk or a twitch here and there, the twin had no life—except, of course, that it could both urinate and develop an erection.

In 1894, at just twenty years old, Laloo fell in love with a German woman whom he had met in Philadelphia at one of his performances. He married her shortly after their meeting and was reportedly very happy with her.

In 1899, there was a demonstration among performers to have freaks be renamed as "prodigies," and Laloo was very visible in the movement. A few years later, Laloo, just thirty-one years old, died. Though some accounts say he succumbed to an unnamed, deadly illness, most concur that he was killed in a train wreck on his way to exhibit in Mexico as a member of the Norris and Rowe Circus. He is buried in Aguascalientes, Mexico.

When beloved Laloo died, he left a very special void that could only be filled in a very specific way. Who knew that at the height of Laloo's popularity, a boy was born and being raised in India, who, eerily enough, had a twin growing from his abdomen? And that when Laloo was gone, there might actually be a suitable replacement?

Piramal Sami is sometimes mistakenly referred to as "Piramal and Sami," with the understanding that Piramal was the man, Sami the headless twin he carried around. But, in reality, this was his first and last name. He was born in Madras, India, in 1888, with a parasitic twin growing from his abdomen. As soon as he could talk and walk, Piramal, against his wishes, was pushed into show business.

At first, he just made appearances in India, where he toured with his dwarf cousin, Soopromanien Munsamy, and pinheads Gondio and Apexia. At the turn of the twentieth century, Piramal headed to America with his entourage. He signed up with Ringling Bros.

and Barnum & Bailey Circus, and, as had been done with Laloo, his twin was dressed and billed as a female.

Piramal stayed with the American sideshow life only for a short time. For one, he had never been comfortable with a performer's lifestyle. Moreover, he didn't trust Americans—and that went especially for the people with whom he worked. Piramal hated the culture and the food, insisting that cooks from India be hired to travel with him to prepare the only cuisine he would eat.

Piramal retired in 1915 and returned to India. No other accounts exist of his life after he left the sideshow.

Frank Lentini

a.k.a. "The Human Tripod"
a.k.a. "The Three-Legged Wonder"
a.k.a. "King of the Freaks"
(1889–1966)

> I think life is beautiful and I enjoy living it.
> —Frank Lentini in his pamphlet "The Life
> and History of Francesco A. Lentini"

Frank Lentini had an infectious personality and was well liked by all the performers he worked with. In addition, he was very popular with audiences, who came in droves not only to look at him and his strange body, but to take in his interesting if irrelevant lectures. Lentini was deemed "King of the Freaks," and this moniker continues nearly forty years after his death.

It's especially interesting that Frank Lentini was so well known, regarded, and understood in his adult life, because his childhood is nearly impossible to follow. Various accounts put his early existence as being somewhere between the happy life of a well-loved son of aristocratic Italian parents and a cast-off—a living, breathing embarrassment to the family, who was abandoned to the care of an aunt whom no one liked. Whatever the truth, not even Lentini himself

Frank Lentini

gives a full picture in his autobiographical pamphlet; he puts himself somewhere in between.

Born Francesco A. Lentini in Rosolini, Siracusa, Sicily, Lentini came into, in one account, a fairly well-to-do family. He was one of twelve children, with seven sisters and four brothers. None of the other children in Frank's family were unique in Frank's special way, and there is no record in the family's history of anyone else being born with extra appendages.

As Lentini himself explains in "The Life and History of Francesco A. Lentini," doctors who examined him over the course of his life said that Lentini's mother "gave birth not to three children, but more than one, yet not three." In other words, the one embryo that became Frank Lentini was originally a trio that fused together in the womb.

Lentini was known as "the Human Tripod" because he was born with three legs. Of course, he didn't actually operate as a tripod because all three legs didn't reach the ground. They did once, but by the time he was about six or seven years old, his third leg stopped growing. Also interesting to note, the two legs that Lentini walked on were not symmetrical, causing him to note: "I have three and yet haven't a pair." In fact, he had four feet and sixteen toes. He also had two sets of sex organs, both fully developed and workable.

As explained previously, there are different accounts of how Lentini ended up in the United States. In one, Lentini was all but abandoned by his parents and shunned by his siblings because of his unusual body. In this version of the tale, a kindly aunt took him in and raised him as one of her own.

Lentini's life story does not unfold so tragically in his own autobiographical pamphlet. He does mention having an aunt who took a special interest in him; however, Lentini never indicates that his parents abandoned him. He writes of their reaction: "Of course it was a great shock to my parents that I was born as I was, but when they found that I was perfectly normal every other way they . . . began to be philosophical about it."

As has been previously stated, it's not always possible to get a wholly accurate history of any of the performers of sideshows. It was not uncommon for them to embellish and fabricate their life stories; the performers were given full license on their cartes de visites to make their life story read any way they wanted. Thus, for many, rewriting one's own history was just part of the game. Therefore, just because Lentini wrote that things happened this way doesn't mean it is factual.

However his childhood went, as an adult, Lentini was generally comfortable with his condition. Although some accounts report that Lentini had consulted physicians to have his third leg removed, and that he was advised not to because it was connected to his spine, most state emphatically that he liked having it and loved how it made him unique.

Frank was a happy and well-adjusted adult, but he didn't always fit in as well as when he was young. Frank himself admitted that when he was a child, he would sit indoors and watch other kids play. This isolation made him depressed, and he considered himself cursed. He was so depressed, in fact, that he would spend most of his time just moping around the house.

Most sources report that Frank's aunt got tired of the boy feeling so sorry for himself and decided to do something about it. She dragged him to an institution—not to commit him, but to give him an eyeful of what the horrible and the miserable really looked like. It changed his life. "I saw a number of blind children and children who were badly crippled and otherwise mistreated by fate," he wrote, "and then and there I realized that my lot wasn't so bad at all. . . . I could hear, talk, understand, appreciate and enjoy the beauties of life. . . . The visit to that institution . . . was the best thing that could have happened to me."

Some records indicate that Lentini was eventually dumped by his aunt and decided to come to the United States just before the turn of the twentieth century to begin his life again. Other accounts say he ran away from his aunt and emigrated to the States in 1898. Lentini says that his entire family moved to America with him; however, they came to seek out a better life for all of them, not just to launch a career for Lentini. In his own account, he says that his father was dead-set against his being in show business, at least until he completed his studies. Lentini was an extremely educated and erudite person; one would have to believe Lentini about this point. He also spoke English, not his first language, impeccably—albeit with a heavy Sicilian accent.

Lentini loved having so much knowledge and he loved imposing it on others. A sizeable chunk of his autobiographical booklet is more a lecture than anything else. After relating his life story, Lentini trails off with various treatises on hygiene, the proper way for women to conduct themselves during pregnancy, the trouble with vices, and everything that's wrong with sex outside of mar-riage—a passage wherein he even quotes Plato: "Virtue is the health, the good habit, the beauty, of the soul; vice is its disease, its bad habit, its deformity."

Lentini also liked talking about himself. People asked him ques-tions about his leg, and he answered them with warmth, honesty, and candor. He explained that his extra appendage never got in his way: he could ride a bicycle, ice-skate, even drive a car. And some-times his third leg was a benefit; when swimming, he used it as a rudder.

Oftentimes, people asked how he dealt with his third leg, as if it were a nuisance. His answer: "If you lived in a world where every-one had just one arm, how would you cope with two?" Another one of his "gimmicks" was to kick a football with his third leg; he could kick a ball clear across the show tent.

When Lentini was thirty, after being a resident of the United States for more than twenty years, he became a citizen. In 1952, Frank Lentini married Theresa Murray and together they had four children: Natale, Frank Jr., James, and Jennie.

At one time, Lentini had become so successful, he even ran his own sideshow. He retired from show business in the early 1960s and moved with his family to Gibsonton, Florida, home of retired freaks. There, he lived out his final days with his family and good friends. Frank Lentini, King of the Freaks, died in 1966.

LEGENDARY IMPRESARIO

ROBERT LEROY RIPLEY
(1893–1949)

Robert LeRoy Ripley was not a sideshow impresario in the traditional sense of the word; however, he was a man with a great passion for oddities—human and otherwise—and made it his life's work to uncover and share all he could find with the world.

In addition to having an insatiable fascination with the strange and unusual, he was also something of a renaissance man. In addition to being an avid collector, Ripley was an artist, a journalist, an author, a radio broadcaster, and a cartoonist. He also pitched one game as a major-league baseball player, but that dream was shattered with an arm injury in his very first game.

Born in California on Christmas Day, 1893, Ripley left the West Coast and his job as a cartoonist at the *San Francisco Chronicle* as a young man to take a job in New York City at the *New York Globe*. In 1918, Ripley started his now-famous Believe It or Not?® cartoons of unbelievable yet utterly true facts. His mission had begun.

Ripley had a passion for travel, and in the 1920s, he traveled to and from Europe and Asia several times, picking up whatever caught his fancy. Soon, his collection got so huge, he needed to house it outside his home, so he opened his first "Odditorium."

Though his "collections" consisted only of objects, Ripley also exhibited people in his Odditoriums, including Bettie Lou Williams (see page 106) and Melvin Burkhart (see page 166).

Ripley died a fairly young man of a heart attack on May 27, 1949.

Bettie Lou Williams

a.k.a. "Lillie B. Williams"

(1932–1955)

> All for love, and nothing for reward.
> —Edmund Spenser, from "The Shepherd's Calendar"

Anyone who knew Bettie Lou Williams remembered her as a kind and generous soul who had an incredible warmth and charm about her—in addition to a parasitic twin growing out of her abdomen. Sadly for Bettie, her loving nature was wasted on the wrong person, and many believe it was her big heart that led to her demise.

Born Lillie B. Williams on January 10, 1932, in Albany, Georgia, Bettie was not born into ideal circumstances. Her parents were poor sharecroppers with plenty more mouths to feed. Perhaps it was lucky that their new baby "twins" only had one mouth, but other issues were pressing. The fear of insurmountable medical bills weighed heavily on them.

And then fate—and fortune—came knocking on their door. In 1933, Dick Best discovered Lillie, who was essentially an infant at the time. He convinced her parents to let him take her to New York City, where she would be able to make them money beyond their wildest imaginations. They agreed to let their little girl go.

Dick Best was thrilled about his new acquisition, and he was going to do whatever he could to make her a star. He changed her name to Bettie Lou Williams and became her first manager. He was exhibiting her at his curio museum in New York City when Robert LeRoy Ripley (see page 105) discovered her. She was by then two years old. After making arrangements with Ripley, Best released Bettie Lou to him. Her first Ripley outing was in 1934 at the World's Fair.

Bettie Lou made $250 per week working for Ripley. Considering that this was during the Great Depression, and that she was a toddler at the time, Bettie Lou was doing just fine—in fact, she was wealthy.

By 1950, Bettie Lou was pulling in more than double her starting wage—besides the $500 or so extra she earned from selling her cartes de visites.

Bettie Lou was perfectly healthy in every respect. The only thing that made people turn their heads was the parasitic twin sister growing from her abdomen. The twin, though considerably smaller than Bettie Lou, grew at the same rate when she was a child but slowed down some as Bettie Lou reached adolescence and adulthood.

When Bettie Lou grew up, she bought her parents a farm with her earnings and built them a house for about $40,000. With her warm and generous spirit, and incredible bank account, she put all twelve of her siblings through college.

Bettie was loved by everyone she came in contact with. She had many suitors who looked past her twin and were rapt with her intelligence and infectious charm; unfortunately for Bettie, she chose the wrong one.

When Bettie was in her early twenties, she fell madly in love with a man who ended up being with her only for her money. They were engaged and he allowed her to spoil him rotten. When he broke up with her and left town, he managed to get away with a sizeable chunk of her savings.

Bettie Lou was devastated. Emotionally, she never recovered. Physically, the rejection also took its toll. Shortly after he left, Bettie Lou died during a vicious asthma attack. She was twenty-three years old.

The romantic version of the story reports that Bettie Lou died of a broken heart; in the more nuts-and-bolts version, however, doctors explained that her death was more likely caused by her twin's head growing into Bettie Lou's lungs, thus causing the obstruction that ultimately killed her.

Ironically, doctors throughout her life told Bettie Lou and her family that her condition would not stand in the way of her leading a normal life; they apparently forgot to mention the complications a twin growing from her abdomen could bring.

EERIE AND ... EXOTIC?

Willie Muse and George Muse

Willie Muse
(c1893–2001)

George Muse
(c1890–1971)
a.k.a. Eko and Iko
a.k.a. "The Men From Mars"

> They were laughing at me. But the joke was
> on them—because they were paying to see me.
>
> —Willie Muse, on his life in the sideshow

Much controversy surrounds George and Willie Muse and their life in the sideshow. Although the above quote denotes that Willie really didn't have a problem with his life and career, his descendents paint a different picture. To them, the Muse brothers were horribly exploited against their will and made to do stupid things in order to line the pockets of their managers with incredible wealth, while the two black albino boys from Roanoke, North Carolina, got nothing.

The reason for this controversy lies in a couple of stories that explain what happened to the boys and how they ended up—and were treated—in the sideshow.

The story that the family of the Muse brothers holds to is that the boys were tricked by bounty hunters and abducted from their home when they were playing in the fields. Apparently, sideshow scouts had heard about the albino black boys who would certainly be a huge draw, and they would stop at nothing, even kidnapping, to get them.

The year was 1899. Showmen were doing well and always looking for the next big thing, and they would pay an enormous reward when they found it. Black albinos were about as odd and rare as snow in the Caribbean, and so they were abducted. The story goes that the kidnapper told the boys that their mother was dead and that they were never going home again.

The other version of the story depicts a very different situation. In this version, it was the boys' mother, Harriet Muse, who sold them to the circus because the family was very poor and was desperate for money. And they weren't small boys at the time they joined up. They were in their late teens and would soon need to be looking for jobs of their own anyway.

From that point on, whether they lived a life of grueling exploitation at the hands of unsavory showmen, or if they were making a living beyond their wildest dreams, is up for debate.

Their manager had them grow out their hair into long white dreadlocks. In 1922, showman Al G. Barnes invited them and their manager to join his circus as he had "quickly realized their possibilities." He promoted them as White Ecuadorian cannibals, Eko and Iko, who were the last remaining specimens from a colony of sheep-headed people. When this flopped, they were renamed "Ambassadors from Mars" in 1923. The claim was that their spaceship had been found in the Mojave Desert.

Eko and Iko traveled all over the country with the Barnes circus, but there was one problem: They were not being paid. Whether this was because they were black, or because management housed, fed, clothed, educated, and taught them to play instruments like the mandolin and guitar, not to mention showing them the world, and that this was payment enough, is also part of the debate. (And don't forget that if it was Harriet who contracted with the circus on her sons' behalf, payment would most likely have been made at the time the deal was made.)

In the mid-1920s, Eko and Iko landed up with Ringling Bros. and Barnum & Bailey Circus. Whatever had happened years earlier, in 1927, Harriet Muse decided to take matters into her own hands. That October, the circus was in town, and because she hadn't seen her boys in more than twenty years, she was determined to go to the circus and bring them home with her. She fought to get them back, but the circus threatened to sue her, stating they were the rightful owners of the "act." Ultimately, Harriet sued back and because the boys had not been paid, she was able to take them back home.

Eko and Iko were excited to go home—in a way. Their dad was already long dead, but their mother wasn't, no matter what they had been tricked into believing. Although they were happy to see her and make up for lost time, the boys sorely missed the action of being on the road and they craved their show business life.

In 1928, their lawyer, who had initially demanded a lump-sum payment of $100,000 from the circus, got them a deal to go back to the circus for $100 cash and $20 a month, in addition to a nice cash settlement. Harriet worked as a maid for $5 per week, so she couldn't deny that extra income would help out considerably, and Eko and Iko went back to work.

The first season they were back, they had twenty-four dates at New York City's Madison Square Garden, and each appearance brought in about 10,000 spectators. This was good news for the brothers, because, as part of their new deal, they were now entitled to sell their own postcards and souvenirs—and keep all the profits for themselves.

In the mid-1930s, Eko and Iko visited Europe, Asia, and Australia on a one-year tour. While on tour, they, in the tradition of great acts before them, performed for royals and dignitaries, including the then–brand new Queen of England.

In 1937, they returned to Ringling Bros., where they worked for several more years. They used some of the money they made to buy their mother a house, where she lived until her death in 1943.

In 1940, Eko and Iko left Ringling Bros to join the Clyde Beatty Circus, where they spent the rest of their careers. Neither brother married, but they each had many dear women friends and perhaps lovers, though this can't be confirmed. They retired in 1961.

Following their retirement, the brothers moved back home, where they shared a house until George died in 1971. Many expected Willie to follow his brother, but they were wrong. Willie lived for many years afterward. For most of the time, he could take care of himself, and spent his days playing his beloved mandolin and reminiscing about the old days.

In 1990, Willie suffered a stroke, which debilitated him only slightly. At nearly a hundred years old, he could no longer play the mandolin, so he learned to play the harmonica.

For the last years of his life, Willie lived on and off in a nursing home and with his devoted grand niece, who spent more then twelve years of her life taking care of him. Willie became very religious in his final years and often repeated the phrase "God is good to me." Ironically, he passed away on Good Friday in 2001 at the astonishing age of 108.

Hiram Davis and Barney Davis

Hiram Davis

(1825–1905)

Barney Davis

(1827–1912)
a.k.a. "The Wild Men of Borneo"
a.k.a. "Waino and Plutano"

> THOUGH DWARFS IN SIZE THEY EXHIBIT GREAT STRENGTH, LIFTING MANY HUNDRED POUNDS IN WEIGHT, or throwing the most scientific six-foot athlete with ease.
> —From the pamphlet for "The Wild Men of Borneo"

The phrase "wild men from Borneo" has become something of a catchall for people who are misbehaving or out of control, but it actually originated as the title of a sideshow act. Ironically, the original "Wild Men," Waino and Plutano, were actually quite well mannered and, well, civilized.

Waino and Plutano were exhibited in the second half of the nineteenth century; they would not be the last of the "Wild Men," however. As noted throughout this book, the "wild man" concept was huge with the Victorians, who were obsessed with savages and exotic lands. This obsession is not unlike certain individuals today who are fascinated by the idea of aliens from outer space.

David and Catherine Davis were originally from England, where their first child, Hiram, was born. When Hiram was about two years old, the family jumped the pond and settled briefly in New York, on Long Island. That wasn't the only thing that happened to the Davises when Hiram was two; at that time they started to notice something was different about their young son.

Also in 1827, the second Davis child, Barney, was born. Much to the continued uneasiness of David and Catherine, even from a very young age, Barney seemed to be different in the same way as his older brother. As they grew, doctors would put names on the differences: "dwarfs" and "imbeciles." Both brothers actually suffered from microcephaly, a rare, neurological disorder in which the circumference of the head is smaller than the average and appears to be almost cone shaped. Mental retardation is almost always the result. Moreover, the boys grew to be only about forty inches tall—just over three feet—and roughly forty-five pounds each.

Just after Barney was born, the Davises moved to a farm in Ohio. There, David and Catherine would have three more children—all normal.

In the late 1840s, David Davis passed away and Catherine remarried. She and her new husband produced a healthy, normal child. It was never learned or understood what caused her to bear two children with a condition that none of her other children shared.

In the early 1850s, when the Davis brothers were in their mid-twenties, they were "discovered" by impresario Lyman Warner.

Hiram Davis and Barney Davis

While his show was in town, he had heard stories of two "midget pinheads" who had incredible physical strength and who lived on a nearby farm. He became determined to get his hands on them for his show, so he rode to the farm to talk with the family and try to cut a deal.

Catherine Davis Porter was appalled at the idea of her children being part of a freak show. She had sheltered her sons as much as she could to protect them from the cruelty in the world, and this man wanted to display them so people could gawk at them? No, she was going to be a tough sell. But after Warner told her about the sums of money the boys could make working in this particular profession, she started to change her mind. Even though the family was in fine shape financially, here was an opportunity for the two eldest children, who had no other prospects, to go out into the world and make their own livings. She acquiesced. Catherine kissed her sons good-bye and entrusted them to Lyman Warner's care.

Warner was beside himself with glee and immediately began building their careers. He billed the brothers as "the Astonishing Wild Men, from the Island of Borneo," and dressed them in savage costumes. They could speak, though not eloquently, but Warner instructed them to speak only in gibberish. And then it was time for the pièce de résistance: their story. Warner weaved an elaborate yarn about how the boys ended up in his custody. He said that they were once actually vicious savages who were captured in Borneo after a horrific fight to the death. In reality, they were reported to be kind, gentle and extremely cooperative and well mannered. But that was none of the public's concern.

Warner set up his wild men for exhibit in dime museums all over the United States and Europe, but he died in 1871, before his investment really took off. Upon his death, his son, Hannaford Warner, took over the management of the wild men. In portraits taken of the Wild Men of Borneo, the younger Warner is included with them; he is the serious, stoic person standing between the boys.

Hiram and Barney were extremely devoted to the elder Warner, but they grew even closer to his successor. They no longer had contact with their original family; according to one account of the lives of the Wild Men, the family filed a petition in 1880 declaring the brothers legally dead.

Also in 1880, the great humbug "discovered" them. Once Barnum got his hands on them, their popularity shot through the roof. When they worked with Barnum, they became one of his most popular attractions.

The Wild Men of Borneo was one of the most successful sideshow attractions of all time. Over the course of their careers, Waino and Plutano pulled in more than $200,000 in earnings. Considering that they started their careers as late as they did, in their mid-twenties, this was quite an accomplishment.

And they worked right up until the end. Hiram got sick in 1903, when he was nearly eighty years old. Still, the wild men went on as much as Hiram could do. When Hiram died in 1905, the curtain came down on the Wild Men from Borneo act. Barney Davis died seven years later.

Both brothers are buried in the same plot in the Mount View Cemetery in Mount Vernon, Ohio. Their gravestone bears the inscription, "little men."

Krao Farini
a.k.a. "The Missing Link"
a.k.a. The Human Monkey"
(1876–1926)

> A little girl of seven, called Krao, who is completely hirsute and presents additional simian characteristics, is being currently exhibited. . . . Her whole body is covered with straight, sleek, black hair; her face is very prognathous; she possesses the ability to project her lips forward almost to the same degree as chimpanzees; she also has prehensile toes which she uses to pick up very small objects from the ground.
>
> —A description of Krao, printed in the
> May 12, 1883, issue of *La Nature*

The Great Farini (see page 118) introduced the world to many strange and unusual acts, not the least peculiar of which was the little girl who had the world convinced a "missing link" between man and beast existed, and that link was her.

According to her bio, Krao killed ten men before she was captured in Africa. Of course this was not true. In reality, she was born in Laos, where her mother worked in the court of the king. Krao was discovered by German explorer Carl Block, who cut a nice deal with her parents to take her to Europe for an exhibition.

Block knew just how to make his money back. He sold Krao to Farini, who became her manager—and eventually, her new father—and wasted no time. When she was about six or seven years old, in 1883, Farini set up a spectacle at the Royal London Aquarium, where he featured Krao, the "scientific and anthropological phenomenon," as the main attraction.

In 1884, Krao was exhibited at the Berlin Aquarium. Here, some unscrupulous show promoters thought it would be a fantastic idea to put her in a cage with "other" apes—the German police did not think so and they were probably right. That anyone could think putting a small human child into a gorilla cage was less an act of stupidity, though, than an act of pure faith. Reportedly, a huge debate raged regarding Krao and whether or not she was fully human. Thus, a case can be made that the promoters truly believed she was one with the gorillas and that the gorillas would see it that way, too.

Darwin's *Origin of Species*, though published about fifteen years before Krao was introduced to Europe and America, was still very much on the minds of people. The pull toward believing in evolution was becoming stronger, and scientists and naturalists alike were intrigued and widely fooled by the little specimen in their raw desire to prove the connection.

Dr. A. H. Keane led the supporters of the group who believed that Krao was, indeed, the missing link they had been searching for. His theory suggested that there existed in the jungles of Laos a race of hirsute people and these people were the bridge between man and beast. That Krao was Laotion was all he needed to know. His examination of her confirmed, beyond a shadow of a doubt, exactly what they had been looking for.

Krao Farini

LEGENDARY IMPRESARIO

GUILLERMO ANTONIO FARINI

**a.k.a. William Leonard Hunt
a.k.a. "The Great Farini"**

(1838–1929)

Like many of the impresarios featured in this collection, the Great Farini was a true renaissance man. In addition to making a name for himself—not to mention a healthy living—as a showman and manager of various acts, he was at one time a circus performer in his own right. Farini also happened to be an inventor—and not just of gaffs—a writer, a businessman, and a painter.

He lived by the mantra "I courted peril because I loved it, because the very thought of it fired my soul with ardour, because it was what others were afraid to face."

Although he was born in Upstate New York, in 1838, Farini was a Canadian. His parents were transplants from Ontario, and the family moved back to Canada, to Bomanville, in the mid-1840s. Farini's birth name was actually William Leonard Hunt, which he would eventually change due to his parents', especially his father's, disapproval of his passion for the circus.

A "passion for peril" began for Hunt when he was thirteen years old and the circus came to Bomanville. He was so taken by what he saw that he immediately set his mind to learning how to perform some of the amazing things he had witnessed.

Of all the tricks he would master, the tightrope would be his earliest claim to fame. He got so good at this that, much to his father's chagrin, he made a name for himself at it. After famed French aerialist Blondin crossed Niagara Falls on a tightrope, Hunt was ripe for the challenge. Hunt used a longer rope at a higher height than had Blondin, and he even performed headstands and somersaults as he crossed. He was a hero.

At this point, Hunt changed his name to Farini, dropped out of the medical school he had been attending, and devoted his life to performing. For years, Farini showcased his tightrope act. He recruited a woman named Mary Olsen to work the rope with him, but, in 1862, she fell to her death. Some speculate that Mary was also Farini's first wife, but that has never been proven. Because of the accident, a few years later Farini invented the net that tightrope walkers to this day still teeter over. Incidentally, Farini also invented the concept of "human cannonball."

Farini continued to tour and perform, taking on a child, known as El Nino, to be his new partner. Farini eventually adopted the child, but this wouldn't be the only time he adopted an act. After he finished performing in 1869, he took on a new role: promoter. One of his stars was Krao Farini (see page 115), a child from Laos whom he also adopted. Another famous person Farini promoted was the heavily tattooed Captain Constentenus (see page 186).

In 1905, Farini retired from show business altogether and moved back to Ontario with his third wife, Anna, in 1921. In 1929, at the age of ninety, he died from influenza.

In contrast, the nonbelievers were led by a Dr. Fauvelle. He, like Keane, was quite anxious to *want* to accept Krao as a missing link, but he possessed a more scientific skepticism about the whole thing. Although he could see that Krao had physical characteristics that were very simian, her grasp of language, acute reflexes, and quick intelligence made him certain that Krao was pure human, afflicted with a condition of severe hirsuteness, and nothing more. She was not a half-ape after all. But despite the proof, Keane refused to accept any other explanation than the one onto which he had glommed.

The novelty of the controversy of Krao's humanity—or lack thereof—never quite wore off. In a 1922 magazine article called "Side-Show Freaks As Seen By Science," Krao, as a freak of nature is dismissed. "There is nothing unusual about her as it is possible for hair to grow anywhere on the human body except on the palms of the hand or on the soles of the feet. More or less growth of hair may be a racial or family trait, or may be due to some stimulant in the hair bulbs."

Some of Krao's simian characteristics were real, and others were "embellished." She did have extraordinarily extended hands and feet with toes so long she could pick up things with them, but she did not actually have, which her bio proclaimed, pouches in her mouth for storing food. Furthermore, there was no proof that Krao's double row of teeth in her mouth were her own or just an extra set she wore when she was on exhibit.

Regardless, Krao Farini was not a savage jungle beast. She was delicate and refined—just covered completely in hair. In the years she was with Farini and touring the world, she learned to speak five languages. She was cultured, educated, and refined. Still, everywhere she went, whether touring the States or the Continent, she was examined by doctors and scientists who were determined to discover some new proof to refute Fauvelle's conclusion.

In the years that followed, Krao toured Europe and spent several years with Ringling Bros. and Barnum & Bailey Circus. She remained one of their biggest attractions. Krao worked in the sideshow right up to her death in 1926, ironically the same year that Zip (see page 121), the other "missing link," passed away.

William Henry Johnson
a.k.a. "What Is It?"
a.k.a. "Zip, the Pinhead"
a.k.a. "The Missing Link"
(1840, 1849, or 1857–1926)

> From the interior of Africa . . . it was captured by a party of adventurers who were in search of the gorilla . . . . they fell in with a race of beings never before discovered. . . . They were in a PERFECTLY NUDE STATE, roving about among the trees and branches,

in the manner common to the monkey and orang
autang . . . the hunters succeeded in capturing three
of these oddities. . . The present one is the only
survivor.

—From a "What Is It?" Advertisement,
New York Herald, March 19, 1860

Zip," Barnum's world-famous "What Is It?" has the distinguished
honor of being known as "dean of the freaks." There were
many reasons for this. For one, although he was advertised as a pinhead, he was much sharper and brighter than your average microcephalic. Moreover, he had a hammy charm, which won over legions
of fans. He was the epitome of the "civil savage," who had a taste for
expensive cigars, an appreciation of couture, and an ability to play up
all sides of the "joke."

Zip was also something of an enigma—no one ever really knew
exactly when he was born. But the main reason that photographer
Matthew Brady bestowed this title upon Zip was that you'd be hard-
pressed to find an act that endured as long as he did, who never
waned in popularity, even long after the death of Barnum.

The first thing to know about Zip was that he was not a native
of the African jungles or the so-called "wilds of California," as
Barnum's ads proclaimed. Nor was he the lone survivor of a tribe
that used to exist along the banks of the River Gamba. He was
William Henry Johnson, a mildly mentally incapacitated man from
Liberty Corners, New Jersey.

The exact date of Zip's birth has remained a mystery. Some
accounts say he was born in the 1840s, which validates the claim
that he was in his eighties when he died. Others say he was born in
the late 1850s. Photos exist of his tombstone and death certificate,
and these cite his date of birth as 1857. But all accounts say he
joined up with Barnum in 1860, so it seems more likely that he was
born in the 1840s and would have been old enough to be exhibited
in the way he was, and not billed as an exotic infant or child.

Another ingredient to toss into the stew is that Johnson wasn't
Barnum's first "What Is It?" That distinction went to British actor

Harvey Leech, whose career was essentially ruined when his fraud-ulence was uncovered. It could be that some accounts have mixed up Leech with Johnson. Regardless, it's a perfect example of how records of sideshow performers cannot always be believed as factual histories.

How did Johnson end up with Barnum? Reportedly, Barnum didn't discover Zip, although he did make him a star. In one version of the story, Johnson was sold into show business by his parents, who were looking to make some quick money. A circus had come to town and showmen had gotten wind of a strange boy who lived there, who had a cone-like head and was said to be mentally slow. This account says Johnson was about four years old at the time he joined the traveling Van Amburgh Circus. Because this was prior to the Civil War, however, Zip's mother wasn't free to sell her off-spring, nor would he be free to be bought. One theory is that due to his size, somewhere just over four feet tall and weighing roughly fifty pounds, and his mental condition, whoever owned the family may have decided he would not be of much use and so sold him into the business. The real truth is lost to history.

However, and whenever, Johnson entered his sideshow life, Barnum hired him when he was already an adult. Darwin's *Origin of Species* had just been published in 1859, and Barnum knew the world was ready to believe in the possibility of a "missing link," a living, breathing bridge between man and ape, and would likely pay a lot of money to see it with their own eyes.

Barnum transformed Johnson by shaving his hair to a point to emphasize the conical shape of his head and dressing him in a suit made with thick black hair, which begged the question of whether or not he was man or monkey. Was this degrading? Absolutely. But it's important to keep history in perspective. At this time, the Civil War was a sneeze away and African Americans had no rights at all. What Zip had, however, that others of his race did not, was a high-paying job and an easy ticket to world-class fame.

Barnum pulled out all the stops for his humbug proof of evolu-tion. In his ads for Zip, he would say things like "Is it a lower order of man? or is it a higher development of the monkey? or is it both in combination? Nothing of the kind has ever been seen before. It is alive, and it is certainly the MOST MARVELOUS CREATURE LIVING."

To keep up the charade, Barnum encouraged Zip never to speak even though he could, and actually paid him an extra dollar a day more when he did not. Zip took Barnum's direction one step further, and instead of being completely silent, he chortled in incoherent gibberish to really maximize the effect.

Zip had lots of gimmicks he invented and put into his act all on his own. One of these was to threaten to "shoot" other acts with a toy pop gun he carried around with him. Later on, he traded in the pop gun for a violin, which he played mercilessly bad and incessantly—until, naturally, patrons would pay him to stop playing. Whether this was a lesson he also learned from Barnum, who, at one time had paid a band to stand outside his American Museum and play badly so people would flee inside the museum to get away from the shrill sounds outside, is not known. But, apparently, his clever maneuver with the violin earned Zip big bucks—about $14,000.

Zip was one of the most popular attractions for all the years he was involved in the sideshow. He was beloved by his audience and fellow performers alike. On April 6, 1914, the *New York World* reported on a birthday party Zip was hosting for himself, and to which other famous freaks had been invited. They had all decided that this would be Zip's sixty-fifth birthday celebration ... though no one, including Zip, considered what his real age—or date of birth—was.

In the last years of his performance, for special occasions, Zip classed up his performance by donning a tuxedo given to him by his then-manager, Capt. O. K. White. It was a suit he loved so much, he was buried in it.

In the 1920s, for the last years of his act, Zip stopped traveling and became a permanent fixture at Coney Island. He didn't mind working there because it was accessible to the chicken farm he had bought in Nutley, New Jersey, where he planned to retire. On April 24, 1926, three weeks after developing a severe case of bronchitis and influenza, Johnson died.

Enigmatic Zip's death brought more questions to the forefront.

For one, it was reported that on his death bed, his last words were: "Well, we fooled 'em a long time." Some have interpreted this to mean that Zip was not mentally challenged at all—that he and Barnum had come up with the ruse and that Zip was likely just a very clever man and talented actor who saw a way to make some big money. Others, however, believe that since Zip was very ill, and probably delirious with fever, he may have been referring only to being the "missing link," which no one had believed for many years anyway.

At his highly attended funeral, which was held at Campbell's Funeral Church on the Upper West Side of Manhattan, his "savage nature" was also called into question. Apparently, he looked like a perfectly normal man in his coffin, dressed in his tuxedo, his silly hairdo completely grown in.

Maximo and Bartola
a.k.a. "The Aztec Children"
(birth and death dates unknown)

> The parties whom Senior [sic] Velasquez first appointed as their temporary guardians brought them to New York via Jamaica, and they will no doubt attract and reward universal attention. They are supposed to be eight and ten years of age, and both are lively, playful and affectionate. But it is as specimens of an absolutely unique and nearly extinct race of mankind, that they claim the attention of physiologists and all men of science.
>
> —From an 1850 account of the expedition that allegedly captured Maximo and Bartola in the wilderness

It would not be a stretch to call Maximo and Bartola the act that paved the way for all other exotic, "ancient race" and "wild man" exhibitions. They were the first pinheads ever to be exhibited in this way. Although they were thought to be wild savage children, the

Maximo and Bartola

last members of the Aztec race, they were in reality just a couple of microcephalic children from South America.

Explorer Ramon Selva brought Maximo and Bartola to the United States, but he didn't capture them at the ruins of an ancient Aztec temple. That was the story created by Barnum. The real truth, as records indicate, was that Selva had been in their village in San Miguel, St. Salvador, in the late 1840s, scouting out exotics when he discovered them. Selva approached their parents, Innocente Burgos and Marina Espina. These simple peasants believed Selva when he said he would take their children with him because he knew someone who could "cure" their condition, and then he would return Maximo and Bartola to them when they were healed. But, as can be imagined, Maximo and Bartola never saw their parents again.

When Selva brought the children to the States, he sold them to a manager known only as "Morris," who first began cooking up their legend. He wrote a forty-eight-page pamphlet outlining the "true" history of these children and how they came to be out with him. The story is long, but the gist of it is that the pair was found on an altar, objects of worship by villagers who believed them to be last of an ancient race of Aztec peoples. With great caution, an explorer was able to extricate them from the tribe and bring them back to the United States.

Morris leased the "children" to Barnum and they were a huge success. Once in Barnum's hands, as was known to happen, their popularity was out of control. Not only did they set and reset box-office records, but, when they were exhibited, a great controversy ensued over whether or not they were authentic. Everyone had an opinion and most people, scientists and naturalists included, believed in their authenticity.

In 1853, Maximo and Bartola toured Europe with Barnum and his entourage as "the Aztec Lilliputians." Upon their return, they were exhibited in Barnum's American Museum, and the controversy continued to fuel the receipts. Eventually, though the mystery was still dripping with controversy, the fervor died down. The act stopped drawing crowds, and Maximo and Bartola went into retirement.

No one heard anything further about them until January 7, 1867, when Maximo and Bartola married each other in London as Senor Maximo Valdez Nunez and Senora Bartola Velasquez. They were allegedly from a culture in which brothers and sisters married to preserve the purity of their pristine bloodline, so not much of a stink was made over the morality of the nuptials.

What happened to Maximo and Bartola after the wedding is simply not known. They pretty much slipped right back into oblivion. Like many of the most successful "exotic" headliners, Maximo and Bartola inspired many others to capitalize on the notion that exotic peoples were out there and the public would fall over themselves just to get a glimpse. Maximo and Bartola may have been the "last of the Aztecs" (and, in fact, in time they wouldn't be *last* as more would eventually be "discovered"), but they were the first of the sideshow exotics. Most every act in this chapter came about because of their success.

Simon Metz
a.k.a. "Schlitzie"
a.k.a. "Maggie, last of the Aztec Children"
(1881–1961)

> Oh, Schlitzie, what a pretty dress. Oh, how
> beautiful you look tonight. . . . You're just a man's
> woman. You know what I mean? Huh? You . . . If
> you're a good girl, when I get to Paris I'm gonna
> buy you a big hat, with a long beautiful feather on
> it. . . . Hasn't Schlitzie got a beautiful dress? Isn't
> that pretty?
> —Phroso the Clown, playfully teasing Schlitzie in *Freaks*

Silly Phroso! Schlitzie was not really a woman. Of course, he very likely knew that. Most who worked with Schlitzie knew he was a man but thought of him as being a woman because he always wore a dress. No, he was not some microcephalic cross-dresser or anything

COURTESY BILL GRIFFITH

Simon Metz

like that. Like most pinheads, Schlitzie was not toilet trained and therefore had to wear a diaper. It was simply easier to "change him" when he wore a dress. His mental age had stopped at three years old, though he lived to be eighty.

Schlitzie is typically a favorite among freak-o-philes. He was warm and silly with a loveable sense of humor. He could barely talk, but when he did, lighthearted, hilarious things came out of him. And even if the audience never understood a word, the light of joy beamed right off his face when someone listened to him.

Reportedly, Schlitzie had a famous hand gesture he was known for. He would tap the palm of one hand with two fingers of the other, saying "You see, you see," when it seemed to anyone else around him that there was nothing at all to be referencing.

Despite his goofy doddering around, Schlitzie was actually quite intelligent for a pinhead. He could count to ten, and sing and dance. And yes, he loved new dresses and hats. He also adored Jackie Cooper, a lot, which had been known to make the actor a wee bit uncomfortable.

Schlitzie was born Simon Metz in 1881. Somewhere down the road, he was given his nickname by the beer company and it just stuck. Some accounts say that Schlitzie was from New Mexico. He came from a family of money and prestige, but because Simon was a blemish on an otherwise perfect existence, he was handed over to the sideshow. Other accounts say that he hailed from a poor farming family in the Yucatan and was discovered by explorers scouting out new oddities. The latter probably rang more true when Schlitzie did a stint as Maggie, last of the Aztec children, but we'll come back to that. What is known is that Schlitzie was not an only child; his sister, Athelia, was also a pinhead. It is believed there were no other siblings.

It is not known how Schlitzie and Athelia were acquired, but showman Pete Kortes became their manager. Somewhere down the line, brother and sister got split up. Athelia stayed with Pete Kortes, and Schlitzie ended up in the hands of George Kortes and his wife. While he was with George Kortes, Schlitzie was exhibited with Barnum. Never one to miss an opportunity, Barnum billed him as

Maggie, last of the Aztec Children, and he exhibited that way for several years.

After his successful run with Barnum, Kortes saw how well he could do by billing Schlitzie as something exotic. Schlitzie became "Astonishing Schlitzie the Pinhead. Not for the faint of heart. Enter this exhibit at your own risk." This was the language of a poster advertising Schlitzie as an exhibit, which is about as far-fetched and hilarious as it gets. Schlitzie continued to travel the world with Kortes as an "astonishing" human oddity, and then another opportunity presented itself.

When Schlitzie was about forty years old, director Tod Browning was looking for circus freaks to cast in the new film he was making about romance gone awry in the sideshow. Browning fell for Schlitzie, as everyone did, and cast him in the film. Schlitzie also fell for Browning. He adored the man like a father, and in cast photos, you can generally always see Schlitzie with his arms around the director. So much did he love Browning that Schlitzie learned to imitate his voice and would bark commands to others on the set.

Schlitzie has more scenes than many of the pinheads featured in the film, his big scene being the back-and-forth he does with Phroso in the beginning quote. But one place you won't see him is the violent finale.

Freaks wasn't Schlitzie's only film. He appeared, uncredited, in *Tomorrow's Children* (1934), an over-the-top screwball-ish dramedy. And in 1941, he was "Princess Betsy," also uncredited, in *Meet Boston Blackie*, the first in a series of *Boston Blackie* films.

George Kortes and Schlitzie eventually joined up with the Canadian Sam Alexander Sideshow. This would prove to be an essential connection for Schlitzie.

When George Kortes passed away, Schlitzie was left in the hands of George's daughter. Unfortunately, she was never much interested in her father's business and had no idea what to do with this "middle aged moo moo wearing man woman child." So she took him to the Los Angeles County Hospital and abandoned him there.

Fortunately, one day a sword swallower who worked in the hospital on the off-season recognized poor lonely and despondent

Schlitzie. He immediately called his boss, Canadian impresario Sam Alexander. Alexander promptly reported to the hospital, begging to have Schlitzie released into his custody, explaining that if the gregarious soul was institutionalized much longer, it would certainly mean a death sentence. Sam Alexander won his plea, and Schlitzie was back in the life he so dearly loved.

Schlitzie retired in the early 1960s and lived out his remaining days in an apartment Alexander had rented for him with a nurse Alexander hired to look after him. Schlitzie died in 1961, after eighty mostly happy years.

Jennie Lee and Elvira Snow

a.k.a. "Pip and Flip"
a.k.a. "The Twins from Yucatan"
a.k.a. "The Wild Australian Children"
(birth and death dates unknown)

> Oh, shame, shame, shame. How many times have I
> told you not to be frightened. Have I not told you
> God looks after all his children?
> —Madame Tetrallini, to her group of "children," in *Freaks*

Not very much has been documented about these adorable pinheads except that they were based at Coney Island, via Samuel Gumpertz (see page 88), for most of their careers and also traveled with the World Circus Sideshow. However, in the early 1930s, these two microcephalic sisters were recruited to work with the cast of *Freaks* (1932); this production gave them a chance to be seen by more spectators than ever before.

The girls' real names were Jennie Lee and Elvira Snow. They were not the same age, and both were very likely born just after the turn of the twentieth century. Although they seemed to be "children" in *Freaks*, because of their size and childlike behavior, their condition made them appear much younger—and, at least in terms

Jennie Lee and Elvira Snow

of mental and emotional development, they were. As Percilla Bejano (see page 196) remembered them in an interview published in James Taylor's *Shocked and Amazed*, "Flip and Pip, the pinheads. . . . You have to put diapers on them or they'll mess up. They're like kids. You have to walk them, take care of them."

Essentially, Pip was as intelligent as a toddler. Flip, who was more sophisticated than her sister, was more on the level of a below-average-intelligence five-year-old. Case in point: Neither was or could be toilet trained and they wore diapers like many other pinheads, like their *Freaks* co-star, Schlitzie (see page 127). Jennie and Elvira, along with Schlitzie and Zip, the What Is It? (see page 121), were the inspiration for the "Zippy" comic by Bill Griffith, started in 1970 and in syndication since 1986.

The girls, who were also at one time or another exhibited as Pipo and Flipo or Pippo and Flippo, in which case they were billed as brother and sister, were managed by their brother, Cliff Snow. He looked after their finances, but left the day-to-day care of them up to others. As Bejano recalled: "They weren't ours. We rented them. A woman had them. She'd change their diapers, see that they eat." What he did secure, however, was a $75 per week fee paid to the family for anyone who wanted to exhibit them.

Even in their childlike innocence, shades of adult jadedness were known to come through every now and then. In *Freaks*, though they weren't in on the climactic violent scene, they still chided Cleo as being "one of us, gooble gobble." And, according to Bejano, "They didn't like police either. They didn't like them. They didn't like the pants they wore or something. Every time they saw them, 'Goddamn cops.'"

After the film, the girls essentially lived out their careers at Coney Island and died in relative obscurity.

HUMAN OR ANIMAL?

Stanley Berent

a.k.a. "Sealo the Seal Boy"

(c. 1925–1984)

> I can actually see the attraction of joining a freak
> show. Sealo managed to support his able-bodied
> family of four and was earning the equivalent of
> five grand a week. I know disabled people today
> that would much rather do that than draw dole and
> be told that they have to undergo another means
> test for incapacity benefit.
>
> —British actor Matt Fraser, who performed a one-act show
> *Sealboy: Freak*, based in part on Berent's life story

Stanley Berent was born into a Catholic family in Pittsburgh, Pennsylvania, sometime in the mid-1920s (the exact date cannot be confirmed). His one sister, reportedly, was physically normal and grew up to become a nun. Many accounts of his life, especially by people who knew him best, always make it a point to emphasize Berent's Catholicism, which likely means that he was a religious fellow. Of course, that's pure speculation.

Berent was afflicted with a condition called phocomelia. He had

EARLYPHOTOS.COM

Sealo the Seal Boy

no arms; he simply had hands that grew from his shoulders. This condition was prominent in the 1950s and 1960s and was linked to expectant mothers who took thalidomide, a drug commonly prescribed to pregnant women to treat morning sickness and as a sleep aid. However, a high rate of birth defects caused its discontinuance for such use. Today, it's generally only prescribed to treat leprosy.

Thalidomide cannot be linked to Berent's condition, however, because the drug was not in use in the 1920s. There is not enough known about Berent's early life to pin down why he was born with phocomelia.

Nevertheless, his affliction did not get in his way. Berent took to sideshows like a seal to water—and that's what he was called, "Sealo, the Seal Boy." He was beloved by fellow acts, promoters, and especially by audiences who adored him as one of the most personable performers ever to grace a sideshow platform. In a message board post, Ward Hall (see page 171) said of Sealo: "In my opinion he sold the most pitch cards of any attraction in the business."

Sealo prized his life in the sideshow, so much so that when "do-gooders" began to take action against the exhibits and their promoters, he fought back, vehemently defending his right to earn a living. But we'll come back to that.

Berent traveled around the United States and the world, even playing in the Caribbean, and he worked with just about every act of his generation during his forty or so years in the business. His performance generally lasted the whole of the show. Once he got up on stage, it was very difficult for him to get down again, so he just stayed. He didn't perform the whole time; he gave his fellow performers a chance to enjoy the spotlight. Generally, he'd just sit in the background, take in the other performances, and enjoy a fine cigar—one of his main pleasures.

Sealo had a simple act. In addition to cracking jokes with his audience, he would show off some of the things he could do despite having no arms. "I can do anything any normal person with regular hands can do," he would say, and it was very true. He shaved his face with a straight razor. He sawed up crates. He smoked cigars. He even inscribed and signed his own cartes de visites. For his pièce de résistance, he would show how he could unzip his pants. It wasn't a pervert maneuver; it was a parlor trick. He would take a stick with a hook at the end and demonstrate his technique. In his own way, he made great strides for the "handi-capable" movement.

Sealo was always involved with people at work; however, after hours, he liked to do his own thing. He always stayed in hotels versus staying on the grounds as most performers are apt to do. He wasn't antisocial; many times he would take in one of his favorite hobbies with his sideshow pals, playing cards, and sometimes he would play well into the night.

For all intents and purposes, Berent led a normal life. He was married and had several children. He made a rather comfortable living—that is, until that was almost whisked away from him by people thinking they were doing him a favor.

In the 1970s, political groups purporting to be looking after the interests of the disabled tried to make sure a law that had been passed several years earlier was taken more seriously. The law basically stated, in effect, that people with disabilities could not be displayed—or display themselves—in public for money. Together with various other acts, including Otis Jordan (see page 83), Berent went to court to fight for his right to make a living.

Shortly after the trial, Berent and his family retired to Gibsonton, Florida, where many of his sideshow friends had already retired. There, he lived out most of his remaining life in the International Independent Showmen's Association Retirement Village. When he became too feeble to properly care for himself, he moved back to Pittsburgh, where he passed away in 1984.

Among classic sideshow acts, Sealo is one that has not been forgotten. His legacy was celebrated recently by British-born Matt Fraser, who was also born with phocomelia. In Fraser's case, thalidomide was the reason. Like Berent and so many before him, Fraser celebrates his right to perform, and the rights of sideshow performers of the past. His "Born Freak," which pays homage to many of these acts, has won many awards, including four "Best of Festival" awards at international disability film festivals. Says Fraser, "I see freak shows as the historical and cultural heritage of the disabled performer. It was the last time disabled performers were welcome on stage by society. After that they were taken away from public view."

Stephan Bibrowski

a.k.a. "Lionel the Lion-Faced Man"

(1891–1932)

> The lion is not so fierce as they paint him.
> —George Herbert

The lion may be king of the beasts, but Lionel the Lion-Faced Man was anything but a beast. He was a perfect gentleman, always impeccably dressed in the finest suits that his money could buy. He was well educated and erudite, and he spoke five languages with fluent eloquence. And, he was covered in a coat of hair that gave him the appearance of looking like a lion.

Even at the time he was born, in 1891, near Warsaw, in Poland, Stephan was covered from head to toe in fine, one-inch-long hair. Neither of his parents had been afflicted with this condition, which was typically hereditary (see JoJo the Dog-Faced Boy, page 144). His mother had a perfectly reasonable explanation for this: Her husband was dead. He had been mauled by a lion, and, much to her horror, she had watched the whole incident unfold before her, all the while she was carrying her son. Through maternal impression, her son had been born looking like a lion. Maternal impression aside, the scientific explanation for his lion-like visage was hypertrichosis, a condition that occurs rarely, but which is always hereditary.

Stephan was discovered at age four by a German impresario known only as "Meyer." His mother, glad to be rid of what she considered an abomination of a child and painful memory of her dead husband, gladly abandoned him into the care of the sideshow. He was exhibited as "Lionel the Lion-Faced Boy."

By the time he started to be on exhibition, his hair had grown to eight inches long on his face and hung about four inches long everywhere else. Lionel was actually almost entirely covered in hair; the only surfaces that were "human" were the palms of his hands and the soles of his feet.

Lionel the Lion-Faced Man

In 1901, Lionel headed to the States and signed up with the Barnum & Bailey Circus. For several years, he toured the world with the "Greatest Show on Earth," also heading back and forth to Europe.

In his act, he showed off impressive gymnastic feats and spoke to the people like the character portrayed by Kelsey Grammer, Frasier Crane, costumed in the suit of a feral feline. Articulate beyond comprehension, he was a very popular attraction. Lionel settled permanently in the United States in 1920. He headed to New York City to become a permanent fixture at Coney Island.

By the late 1920s, Lionel grew weary of American sideshow life and retired to Germany. He reportedly died in Berlin of a heart attack in 1932 at the age of forty.

The Feejee Mermaid
a.k.a. "The Fiji Mermaid"
(1822–1865)

> Shall I part my hair behind? Do I dare to eat a peach?
> I shall wear white flannel trousers, and walk upon
>   the beach.
> I have heard the mermaids singing, each to each.
> I do not think that they will sing to me.
> —T. S. Eliot, "The Love Song of J. Alfred Prufrock"

P. T. Barnum usually receives the credit for introducing the Feejee Mermaid to the world, but it was actually not his invention. In fact, many years before Barnum would begin his quest to dazzle and delight with oddities and rarities, the Feejee Mermaid had already been astounding European audiences.

The mermaid itself was not exactly what might come to mind when one thinks of what a mermaid should look like—a siren of the sea, with the torso, face, and hair of a goddess—like beauty, with a sleek, sinuous, and shiny aquamarine tail. One look at the picture dismisses that image immediately. This taxidermed thing was just

AUTHOR'S COLLECTION

The Feejee Mermaid

under three feet long. Its overgrown head was partially covered by a rug of thick, coarse, black hair. The face was contorted, but its features resembled that of a human face—a nearly indescribable human face, that is. The tail began just below the sagging breasts, and it was generally described as looking like a salmon with the head cut off.

Remember, this period was just on the crux of Darwin and his controversial theories of evolution. For that reason, naturalists jumped on the chance to examine the sapien-fish. And while doubt mixed heartily with the findings of these new scientists, the public was still prepared and excited to pay their coin for a chance to gawk at what they wanted to believe was a miracle of nature.

The first exhibitor of the "Feejee Mermaid" was an American sea captain named Samuel Barret Eades. So excited was he when he encountered the specimen of what he believed to be a mermaid when he was conducting business in the Dutch West Indies, that he immediately had to have it. According to the merchant who sold it to him, the mermaid had recently been caught off the coast of Japan. It could have been discovered in a back alley in Chinatown for all he cared. What he saw in the mermaid was a chance to make some money. Of course, he didn't have any of his own money at the time. . . .

Captain Eades had a brainstorm: He would sell the vessel he had been operating and use the money to purchase the mermaid. Of course, the ship did not fully belong to him; it was well over three-fourths owned by British merchant Stephen Ellery. But that was purely incidental. Eades was sure that the mermaid would bring him such fame and fortune that the $6,000 he pocketed for the purchase of the boat would be easily reimbursable—if he chose to reimburse it.

Proud purchase in tow, the gullible sea captain with the dollar signs in his eyes headed back to London after hitching a ride on another vessel, his prized gaff in tow. When the boat docked, however, his plans were stalled when the mermaid was confiscated at customs.

Within a couple of weeks, he got his mermaid back. All the while, Eades made a pre-Barnumesque play at getting his mermaid noticed. He ran ads in all the local papers, touting his lusus naturae as the most exciting and important discovery ever made.

Eades garnered much interest—including that of Stephen Ellery, the owner of the vessel Eades had hocked to nab his prize. Upon confrontation, Eades not only refused to give Ellery his money back, he told him that if Ellery kept after him, he would have no choice but to flee England. Ellery didn't become a successful businessman because he was a dummy. He got the law on his side and quickly grounded Eades's money-making mission.

After intense investigation from naturalists, it was ultimately determined that Eades's mermaid was a fraud—albeit an excellent one. The top portion was the body of an orangutan; the bottom a large salmon. While no seam could be discerned as to where the monkey ended and the fish began, the specimen was obviously filled with artificial stuffing and carefully sewn together by expert hands.

Despite the findings, crowds continued to pay to view the mermaid; that is, until the novelty wore off. In 1823, the exhibit was closed down. No one cared about it anymore by 1825, and Eades's career as an impresario was over. He spent the rest of his life working for free to pay off his impulse buy.

Of course, that wasn't the end of the mermaid's career. In 1842, Boston Museum curator Moses Kimball was contacted by an Englishman who had inherited a most unusual object from his father. Upon inspecting the specimen, Kimball contacted his good friend Barnum in New York. Barnum was equally impressed. Kimball bought the fish thing for a song, and he and Barnum went about exhibiting it. Barnum named the thing "the Feejee Mermaid," made up a story about how it was captured in the Fiji Islands, and hence, Barnum's most famous humbug was born.

In what would later be labeled a famous publicity stunt, Barnum contacted newspapers and gave them each different "exclusive" pictures of what the mermaid looked like. A faux naturist was "hired" to act as the mermaid's manager.

Within a couple of years, once New Yorkers got bored of it, Barnum sent his mermaid on a whirlwind tour of the south—which ended badly and the mermaid had to be sent back to New York.

The last anyone knew of Eades and Barnum's special mermaid, it was lost in the rubble of the American Museum during the great fire of 1865. While other incarnations of the mermaid have surfaced, the original is nothing more than a fond yet fraudulent memory and a long-since-cleared-away pile of dust.

Fedor Jeftichew

a.k.a. "JoJo the Dog-Faced Boy"

(1868–1903)

> The most prodigious paradigm of all prodigies
> secured by P. T. Barnum in 50 years. The Human
> Skye-Terrier the crowing mystery of nature's
> contradictions.
>
> —from P. T. Barnum's write-up of JoJo

Unlike Lionel, the Lion-Faced Man (see page 138), JoJo the Dog-Faced boy reportedly played into the savage nature of his character, at least when he was younger. Later, it was usually his father who played the angry savage, and JoJo who played Dad's more dignified foil.

When he stopped working with Dad, JoJo dressed in the finest clothes and learned to speak three languages: Russian, English, and German. He was five feet, eight inches tall and entirely covered in hair, giving him the appearance of a Skye terrier, and murking that line between beast and man that Barnum was always so excited about.

Fedor Jeftichew was not born in the wild. Although Barnum said that a hunter found JoJo on expedition in the deep, dark, wild forests of Kostroma in Central Russia, this wasn't at all true. JoJo was discovered in London, England, by Charles Reynolds. At the time, JoJo had been performing with his father and Reynolds could see that there was potential far past what they were doing. It was Reynolds who brought JoJo to the States and introduced him to Barnum; it was Barnum who hit the ground running with the unusual exhibit and created all the hype.

"[JoJo] was found in company with his Dog-Faced Father," reads the explanation of how JoJo came to Barnum in JoJo's pamphlet. "They were first discovered by a hunter, and a party was formed who tracked them to their cave, and, after a desperate conflict, in which the savage father fought with all the fury of an enraged mastiff, their capture was effected."

JoJo the Dog-Faced Boy

JoJo the Dog-Faced Boy was not from a race of dog people from the wilderness of Kostroma. He was a boy afflicted with hypertrichosis, a condition of excessive hirsuteness, which is typically hereditary and reportedly quite rare. At the time JoJo was famous, there had been only twenty-four reported cases in a period of about 300 years. And he was born in St. Petersburg, Russia.

JoJo toured for several years before retiring and died of pneumonia when he was just thirty-five years old.

Grace McDaniels

a.k.a. "The Mule-Faced Woman"
a.k.a. "The Ugliest Woman in the World"
(1888–1958)

> See Grace McDaniels, the mule faced woman
> And she's the homeliest woman in the world.
> —Tom Waits, "Lucky Day Overture"

A picture in and of itself cannot portray exactly what poor Grace McDaniels actually looked like, and because all pictures taken of her have essentially been in black and white, the actual effect is lost to time. The only way to really understand the kind of horrible facial atrocity inflicted on this otherwise pleasant, kindly, warm, and gentle human being is to understand it through the eyes of people who knew her.

"The first time I met Grace McDaniels was at the store show," said Percilla "Monkey Girl" Bejano (see page 196), in *Shocked and Amazed*. "I went down to the museum, sat down and started to eat my breakfast and across was Grace McDaniels. She almost made me sick, the first time I saw her. . . . She was nice though." Dolly "the Ossified Girl" Regan remembered, in *Freak Show Man*: "When I first met Grace McDaniels, the 'mule-faced woman,' I fainted. Of course, I felt terribly bad about it later as Grace was the kindliest person in the world."

Reportedly, Grace's face resembled a squished handful of raw ground beef. And beneath the skin condition were no redeeming features. Her nose sat on her face like a rotten pineapple. Her deep-set eyes sunk far into her head like two raisins in a lump of raw dough. Completing the effect was a pair of grotesquely bloated lips, which defy any kind of metaphoric explanation.

There was no competition when Grace McDaniels entered a "world's ugliest woman" contest while attending a visiting carnival with friends when she was young. While her moniker would later be changed to "the Mule-Faced Woman," a term she felt infinitely more comfortable with, she began her career in showbiz labeled with her contest-win title as her name.

It may be presumed that Grace McDaniels had no one—no friends, family, or suitors—because of her condition, but that would be wrong. Grace had an incredibly sweet and generous nature, and readily made friends everywhere she went. Once people got past what was on the outside, the inside was a pure gift of humanity. Not only did she make many friends, but she kept them. Unfortunately, her indelibly sweet nature also made her quite easy to take advantage of, which happened with unscrupulous managers from time to time, and especially with her most crooked manager, her son, Elmer.

Differing accounts denote how Grace McDaniels ended up with a son. Some say that she had been married, but that her husband ran off when she became pregnant, terrified that his offspring would take after his wife. Others say that she had many suitors, but never actually wanted to settle down with any one man. A most disturbing account of how Elmer came to be, however, involved Grace being attacked and raped by a carny worker one night after the show. The story changed with every account.

One thing that remains consistent, however, is that she named her son Elmer, and, in her eyes, he could do no wrong. When he was old enough, she even made him her manager. Unfortunately for Grace, her son was a drunk and a ne'er-do-well. In addition to stealing from her and ruining her financially, he also pretty much destroyed her career by viciously fighting with showmen who would have given Grace work if it had not been for her son.

Elmer eventually drank himself to death in 1958. Grace was done with the business at this time and so no need to hire a new manager. The grief she felt for her dead son ultimately proved to be too much for her, and within a few months of his death, Grace perished in August 1958.

Joseph Carey Merrick

a.k.a. "The Elephant Man"
a.k.a. "John Merrick"

(1862–1890)

> 'Tis true my form is something odd,
> but blaming me is blaming God.
> Could I create myself anew,
> I would not fail in pleasing you.
>
> If I could reach from pole to pole
> Or grasp the ocean with a span,
> I would be measured by the soul;
> The mind's the standard of the man.
>
> —A poem Joseph Merrick quoted often (The attribution
> for this poem is unknown; it is believed to be Carey's
> original verse, but this has never been documented.)

When he returned from his first meeting with Joseph Carey Merrick, Dr. Frederick Treves called the poor man "the most disgusting specimen of humanity. . . . At no time had I met with such a degraded or perverted version of a human being as this lone figure displayed." That was before he got to know him. When he did, and when the rest of the world who once feared him got to know him, they saw a warm, intelligent, and sensitive human being, not a monster.

Much like the Phantom of the Opera, Merrick was a channel of beauty behind a hideous façade; much like the biblical Job, he was a "punching bag" of misfortunes God had somehow inflicted all in one place. He was a man desperate to love life, if only he could be given a break.

For the most part, the sideshow entertainers in this collection openly chose to exhibit themselves for money and fame. With the exception of the pinheads showcased in chapter 5, and various others, whose motives are questionable, most embraced the "carny" lifestyle as not only an alternative to being institutionalized, but as a way to shine from their oddities instead of being crushed by them. Most never suffered adversity because of their particular afflictions; most flourished. Of course, there are always exceptions.

Like Robert Wadlow (see page 33), Joseph Merrick, who noted Merrick biographers Howell and Ford have most cleverly and succinctly coined an "Urban Caliban," turned to the pre-carnival back alley as a last resort to making a living. But very much unlike Robert, whose relatives even today protect and preserve his reputation and dignity like a pack of lions, Joseph, for most of his life, had no one who cared about him. Also like Robert Wadlow, when most people write about Merrick, his association with the sideshow aspect of his life is incidental. But, arguably, Merrick's days as a sideshow attraction were pivotal in his "transformation" in the eyes of the world.

It can't be ignored that Merrick was a tragic figure—perhaps the most tragic of all. Of all the tragedies that surround this enigmatic figure, the first is that Joseph Merrick was completely normal when he came into the world on August 5, 1862. (It should be noted that his name was Joseph, not John. Dr. Treves, in his later writing named him "John," but the reason for this is not known. It should also be noted that Merrick, himself, cited his year of birth as 1860, though his birth certificate said 1862.)

Merrick was born in Leicester, England, to Mary Jane Potterton, who was crippled, and her husband, Joseph Rockley Merrick, a warehouseman. Joseph and Mary Jane were married when Mary Jane was twenty-six years old and already pregnant with her son. Shortly after the marriage, Joseph switched professions to work in a cotton factory to make a better living for his new family.

During her pregnancy, Mary Jane was reportedly run over by an elephant that had gotten loose from a local carnival. No report of such an incident is recorded in the period in which she was pregnant, but it's entirely possible that such a report might be lost to time. In any case, three months later, Joseph was born. Doctors, scientists, and promoters alike would later use this incident to blame Merrick's condition on maternal impression: The pregnant Mary Jane Merrick was attacked by an elephant, and therefore her son became the "Elephant Man." Again, this would not come to pass right away.

Joseph was normal until the age of five, then his lower lip began to swell. Shortly thereafter, he suffered a bad fall, which damaged his hip and ensured he never walked properly again. Things essentially went downhill from there.

A couple of years later, Mary Jane and Joseph had another son, who was normal, but who would die young. When he was five years old, he contracted scarlet fever and didn't survive. A third child, this time a girl, was born a couple of years after that loss, and, like her mother, she was also crippled.

In the midst of all of this, Joseph's condition became ever worse. He began to be shunned by everyone around him—with the exception of his mother. Mary Jane always adored her homely boy and did whatever she could to protect him from the world and a fate that seemed to get worse by the day. But then, the biggest tragedy of all occurred: In 1873, Mary Jane developed bronchial pneumonia and died.

Devastated and unable to properly care for his family, Joseph's father married their landlady shortly after Mary Jane's death. The landlady had never been a fan of young Merrick, to say the least. Now, as he was her stepson, it was worse. Every day she did something vicious and wicked to Merrick and made it increasingly difficult for him to live with them.

Merrick did whatever he could to stay in his stepmother's good graces and tried to pull his weight around the house as best he could. In 1875, he got a job in a cigar factory, but this was short-lived. The swelling deformity on his hands made it nearly impossible for him to properly roll the paper around the tobacco. Next, he got a job as a door-to-door salesman for men's shoe polish and clothing. It doesn't take a Ph.D. to realize that Merrick wouldn't do well as a salesman.

Eventually came the ultimatum: Joseph's evil stepmother told her husband that he was going to have to choose between his own son and her. Because the elder Joseph relied on his wife for lodging and to help care for his crippled daughter, not to mention that he had never been particularly fond of his unusual son, there was no question who was going to have to go.

Joseph left home and tried to fend for himself in the streets, but to no great success. Fortunately, he was going to have some help. In 1879, a compassionate uncle, known only as Charles, and his wife, Jane, got wind of what happened to their nephew. Charles combed the streets looking for him. When he found the poor boy, he talked him into moving in with his family.

In the late 1870s, times were tough for working folk. Merrick began to see the extra strain on his uncle's family, and, after Christmas one year, left the small apartment and signed himself into the Leicester Union Workhouse. He stayed there only a short while—this time. Merrick felt like he was taking up space for someone who might be more worthy, and he signed himself out after six days. Unfortunately, Merrick's deformities continued to advance and, in lieu of starving to death on the streets, he had to return to the workhouse for several more weeks.

In his own autobiography, Joseph later explained what had happened to him. "My feet and legs are covered with thick, lumpy skin, also my body," he explained, "like that of an elephant, and almost the same colour, in fact, no one would believe it until they saw it, that such a thing could exist."

As if things couldn't get worse—and in the case of Joseph "Job" Merrick, it's absolute folly to assume that things would not—they did. By 1882, his deformities had advanced so menacingly that they threatened to close off his throat completely. He required surgery.

While Merrick was recovering, he found out about a way that people like him could make a living. He wrote a letter to Sam Torr, a noted promoter, explaining the details of his condition, in the hopes that he could display himself as an attraction and make some money. Soon, he secured a meeting. Upon seeing Merrick, Torr and his colleagues were convinced Joseph would be a hit. They put him under the management of impresario Tom Norman (see page 155), who became a kind of "fairy godfather" to the young Merrick.

To anyone who's seen the David Lynch film *The Elephant Man*, this probably sounds like a bunch of hooey; it's not. In recent years, Norman has been vilified, but in actuality, he was never the bad guy he was depicted as in the movie. In his own autobiography, Norman reported that "The big majority of showmen are in the habit of treating their novelties as human beings, and in a large number of cases, as one of their own and not like beasts." And it is a fact that Norman treated Merrick with dignity and respect. Joseph kept all the proceeds from his postcards. Of course, Norman had to "sell" Merrick, and he did even that with respect, touting: "The Elephant Man is not here to frighten you but to enlighten you."

In 1884, Dr. Frederick Treves first met John Merrick. He was decidedly less accepting than Norman had been, as evidenced by his initial reaction: "This fact—that it was still human—was the most repellent attribute of the creature."

Treves had come to see Merrick on the recommendation of another doctor. When he was through, he wanted to study him, and Treves gave Merrick his calling card. That year, Treves presented Merrick to the London Pathological Society, and then again in 1885. It was like another exhibition, but this time, there was nothing in it for Merrick except to be gawked and prodded at. Which was worse?

Treves explained to his colleagues of Joseph that "from the brow, there projected a huge bony mass like a loaf, while from the back of the head hung a bag of spongy, fungous looking skin." The doctors in Treves's organization surmised that the condition was elephantiasis, a disease that is parasitical in nature, and which was easily explained with the maternal impression theory. What scientists now believe is that Merrick suffered from Proteus syndrome, of which fewer than 100 documented cases have ever been reported. In July 2003, tests of Merrick's DNA from Merrick's hair and bone confirmed that what he suffered from was most probably Proteus and perhaps type 1 neurofibromatosis.

Joseph Merrick's entire body was affected. From head to toe, he was covered in cauliflower-type warts that emitted an incredibly offensive odor. The only parts that were spared were his left arm, which was delicate and feminine; a small section of his face, including his eyelids and earlobes; and his genitalia. His fingernails were also perfect. Aside from his affliction, he was healthy and strong, though he stood just over five feet, two inches tall.

Merrick stayed with Norman as long as he could, but was forced to hit the road when the police started to bust up the display. He got an opportunity to travel as an exhibit, but this was to be an ill-fated scam. Somehow, he landed in the unscrupulous hands of an evil manager (some say he had an Italian name, like Ferrari), who took him to Belgium, robbed all the money he had made working with Norman, and left him stranded to die.

Ever a fighter, Merrick miraculously made his way back to London. Without any money and looking the way Merrick did, and having to hide from people every step of the way, his journey was undoubtedly grueling, but eventually he arrived back at the Liverpool train station.

He nearly passed out upon arrival, right in the middle of the train station. As luck would have it, someone found Treves's calling card on Merrick's person, so Treves was immediately summoned.

Merrick was taken to Whitechapel Hospital, where he would live out his days in basement rooms—initially in seclusion, but then with regular visitors. In his time there, all who came in contact with him learned that he was not a monster at all; he was gentle and kind. He even built models of buildings with the nurses.

Treves initially thought Merrick was "an imbecile and had been an imbecile from birth," but when he got to know him, he realized nothing could be further from the truth. He learned that Merrick could actually speak quite eloquently, but the words were muffled by the deformity of his mouth.

Even so, he was an outsider. Most of the time, Merrick took solace in books. He could be miserable and depressed until his Sunday afternoon chats with Treves. Over the years, his relationship with Treves blossomed; however, he still remained a pained outsider, wanting so desperately to be normal and be let "in."

One year for Christmas, Treves asked Merrick what he wanted. Always fancying that he could have the life of a great and distinguished gentleman, Merrick asked for a shaving set he had seen in a men's magazine. Of course, he could never use it; he simply liked to take the components of the case, fondle them, and dream.

Childlike in his passions, Merrick was like an adolescent boy in his reverence for women. Of course, women had never looked at Merrick with anything but scorn. One day, Treves introduced Merrick to a beautiful widow, who shook his hand and smiled at him. This opened up his world for him. The event caused him to break down and cry, but it was a crucial stepping stone for him. From that day, he started going out and talking with people, and even took in the theater. "In making my first appearance before the public, who have treated me well—in fact I may say I am as comfortable now as I was uncomfortable before."

Over the years, Merrick had many admirers, including the Prince and Princess of Wales, who were frequent visitors, and an actress, known only as Mrs. Kendal, who wrote often and sent gifts. He even started to become something of a celebrity, though his happiness would be short-lived.

Joseph Carey Merrick passed away in his sleep on April 11, 1890. He was only twenty-seven years old. The cause of death was ruled as asphyxiation, and there was some controversy concerning his demise. A brief investigation concluded that he hadn't been murdered as many had thought. The reason he died was related to his wanting to be normal. After his death, Treves commented that "[Merrick] often said to me that he wished he could lie down to sleep, 'like other people.'" It was surmised that Merrick had done just that, and died trying.

Immediately afterward, Merrick's remains were cast in plaster. Contrary to popular belief, Michael Jackson does not own the bones of the Elephant Man. Today Joseph Carey Merrick's skeleton resides in a British museum, where it continues to be a source of curiosity and a reminder that life is never quite as bad as you may imagine it is.

LEGENDARY IMPRESARIO

TOM NORMAN

a.k.a. "The Silver King"
(c. 1850–1930)

A late-on-the-scene contemporary of P. T. Barnum, Tom Norman was known as "the Silver King," not because he was some kind of pirate who was interested only in making money at any cost. He was named as such by Barnum when they met because Norman wore lots of silver jewelry.

That's the problem with poor Tom Norman. He will likely always be remembered as the vicious sadist who exploited the pathetically fated Joseph Carey Merrick (see page 148) while he profited at his expense. That's a fabrication of Hollywood; Norman was actually quite kind and caring and always respectful of Merrick and his other acts. He was humane and also very resourceful, and had a pretty successful career as a showman.

In the 1870s, Norman, who typically exhibited his acts in abandoned store fronts, started his career with a woman known as the Skeleton Woman. Indeed, as Norman writes in his autobiography, "You could exhibit anything in those days. Yes anything from a needle to an anchor, a flea to an elephant, a bloater you could exhibit as a whale. It was not the show; it was the tale that you told." He wasn't the first showman who made a buck this way; he certainly would not be the last.

Not much is known about Norman after his time with Merrick, except that he made a good living exhibiting unusual specimens right up until his death in 1930.

Julia Pastrana

a.k.a. "The Ape Woman"
a.k.a. "The Baboon Lady"
a.k.a. "The Bear Woman"
a.k.a. "The Marvelous Hybrid"

(1834–1860)

> Her features were simply hideous on account of the
> profusion of hair growing on her forehead, and her
> black beard; but her figure was exceedingly good and
> graceful, and her tiny foot and well-turned ankle . . .
> perfection itself.
>
> —Naturalist Frank Buckland of Julia Pastrana

Without a doubt, Julia Pastrana is one of the most fascinating human curiosities of all time. In her life, she was an accomplished performer and, in her way, a woman of the world who spoke her native language as well as fluent English and Spanish. Even in her death, as you will see, Julia continued to draw crowds.

More than a hundred years after her death, a movie was made about Julia's unique life, and, well, afterlife; at the time of this writing, a second film is in the works, which, at one time, had even attracted Richard Gere to star as Julia's manager husband.

But underneath all the hair and the facial deformities, Julia was just a regular woman who wanted what most women want out of life—and who, without a doubt, fell in love with the wrong man.

Julia was born a Mexican Indian into the Root-Digger tribe. From birth, she was covered in a blanket of thick black hair and was shunned by everyone except her mother. When her mother died, she was all but disowned by her family and her tribe and regarded as an orphan.

But the unusual girl was known throughout Mexico; instead of being sent off to live in an orphanage, Governor Pedro Sanchez, who had a curious fascination with her, invited Julia to live with him and his family, where she pulled her weight as a servant in their house.

Julia Pastrana

Julia hated working in the governor's house, where she was treated as a spectacle and an animal. She had had enough by the mid-1850s and decided to head home, where at least she had some kin to mistreat her.

On her journey, young Julia did a fair amount of soul searching. She was going back to her tribe because it was the only life she had really ever known, but what was there for her? With her mother gone, the answer was nothing.

As luck, or more like it, fate, would have it, Julia never made it home. On her journey, she was intercepted by an American scout. He couldn't believe his good fortune in having found this wandering wonder of nature, and he talked her ear off about how she could head to the States and make an incredible living. With no one keeping her in Mexico, she decided she had nothing to lose and she went with him.

Pastrana's career officially got off the ground in 1854, in New York City, where she was exhibited at the Gothic Hall museum. Billed as "the Ape Woman," she was a standout among the other curiosities. Over time, her act became more than her just standing there and being gawked at. With lessons, she learned to dance and sing, and, reportedly, she had the voice of an angel, an incredible mezzo soprano that intoxicated all who heard her sing. Julia traveled with the show all over the United States and Europe, and made new fans everywhere she went.

There was no reason people should not be taken by the four-foot, six-inch, 120-pound curiosity. She was always pleasant and cheerful and always gave a great show. Though, not everyone was so enamored. In 1857, German officials forbade her to perform in their country as they deemed her an obscene spectacle. But they were a small trickle of dissent in a vast sea of good favor.

Soon, Julia fell under the management of impresario Theodore Lent, who made sure she had plenty of exposure, and, with his skills for sensationalism, Julia's fame and renown only soared.

Scientists and naturalists were just a couple of the groups that couldn't get enough of Julia. It has been speculated that Julia was examined by scientists almost as much as by spectators.

Another group that couldn't get their fill of the sexpot oddity were potential suitors. Men fell all over themselves to possess her. Lent made sure his prize didn't fall under anyone else's control; he proposed to her. Because of her deep devotion to him for looking out for her and her career, she accepted. They were married in 1858. She was madly in love with him and never imagined that the feeling was not as strong on his end.

Because of her animal-like visage, Julia Pastrana was thought to be illiterate, but this was not true. Aside from her association with her husband, who took her out every now and then provided she wore a thick veil so that no one could see her for free, Julia really didn't have much of a social network off the stage. As a way to fill her typically lonely days, she buried herself in books. (Ironically, the only way she would ever be buried, even after her death.)

In 1859, Julia learned she was pregnant. She was overjoyed, as was Lent, who was hoping to bring a new source of income into the world. Julia went into labor on March 20, 1860. Much to her disappointment—and Lent's glee—their son was born hairy and deformed like his mother. He died within a couple of days. Julia died a few days later, on March 25, 1860, of peritonitis. Her last words: "I die happy; I know I have been loved for myself."

This, however, was not the end of her career. Far from it, actually. And it was only the beginning of her son's sideshow career.

The greedy bastard that he was, Lent sold the bodies of his wife and son to a Moscow professor, who performed a miracle of embalming on the bodies. When Lent learned about how perfect the bodies were, and that the professor was exhibiting them in the interest of science, he bought them back.

In 1862, in London, Julia Pastrana began her "come back (from the dead, that is) tour" as Lent dragged and paraded her and her son's mummies throughout Europe.

In 1864, Lent remarried—another bearded lady. He exhibited her as Zenora Pastrana, passing her off as Julia's sister. When Zenora tired of the competition from her husband's dead wife and son, the mummies were leant, for a price, of course, to various universities and museums.

In 1884, Lent literally lost his mind. He died in an insane asylum later that year. His second wife took the mummies with her on her travels and exhibited them in her act. In 1889, she got tired of her husband's dead wife and child and gave them away.

For the next hundred-plus years, the bodies changed hands so many times, it would be tedious to list them all here. They were exhibited in sideshows, they were exhibited in museums. At one point, they were stolen and vandalized. The body of Julia's son has been gone a long time, eaten by mice in the 1980s. Today, Julia's mummy, still pretty much intact, rests in storage in Oslo, never to be exhibited again.

Yes, it was an unusual life, but an even stranger death. Julia Pastrana only lived about twenty-six years, and, of that time, only exhibited herself for less than 10 years; as a mummy, she traveled around the world for an additional 130 years.

Grady Stiles Jr.
a.k.a. "The Lobster Boy"
a.k.a. "The Lobster Man"
(1937–1993)

> People try to put us all into the same bunch, saying
> "if you're a 'freak' you're bitter and angry at life."
> Well, you can't classify us. Some enjoy and love
> people. Some are resentful and feel God played
> them a dirty trick.
>
> —Half-girl Jeanie Tomaini, to *USA Today*, in reference
> to Grady Stiles after his wife's murder trial

Grady Stiles Jr. is perhaps the most controversial sideshow performer who ever lived. In this book, he is the only convicted murderer. He is also the only one in this assemblage who has ever *been* murdered. But was the "Lobster Boy" truly a "victim of society"—or was society his victim?

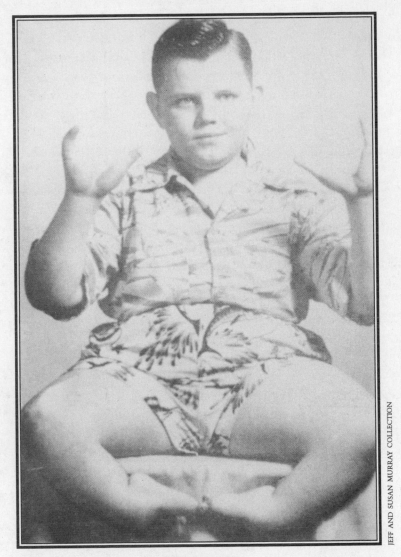

JEFF AND SUSAN MURRAY COLLECTION

Grady Stiles Jr.

The infamous teratological tyrant was born in Pittsburgh, Pennsylvania, on July 18, 1937. Like his father, Grady Sr., Grady Jr. was afflicted with ectrodactyly, a condition that occurs about once in every 90,000 births, and which is hereditary. The Stiles family has five incidences over the generations. Not only did Grady and his father have it, but also Grady's grandfather and Grady's son and daughter.

In ectrodactyly, the afflicted has no fingers; instead, the hands are divided like claws. While it doesn't occur in every case of the unusual condition, in Grady's case, his legs were also deformed. They were curled at the bottom with no feet, making walking impossible. For the most part, Grady rode around in a wheelchair, but he could move himself around without it with his incredibly strong "hands" and arms.

Grady Stiles Sr. brought his son into the sideshow business when he was just seven years old. For the next few years, "the Lobster Family" traveled with several outfits, including the Lorow Bros. Sideshows and Royal American Shows, where he first met Ward Hall (see page 171). Stiles was a teenager by this time, and this is when he broke away from his dad.

Said Hall in an *Amusement Business* article in December 1992, "Grady went out on his own . . . when Floyd Gooding [Gooding's Amusement Co.] built a sideshow for him." Grady was the big-time now. Grady had lots of power. And Grady let it get to his head.

When he was working with this show, Grady met Maria Teresa Herzog. She was uncontrollably smitten by his personal magnetism, as she confessed in the A&E *City Confidential* documentary called "Gibsonton."

Within months, they were married. Soon, they would add two children to their family. Their oldest daughter, Donna, did not inherit ectrodactyly, but their next daughter, Cathy, did. This was great news to Grady and he doted on his protégé. When he felt that she was old enough, he took her into show business with him, just as his father had done with him.

Things were okay for the young family for only a short while. Grady had a dark side, and when he drank, he was known to become very abusive to his family. Wheelchair and claw hands did not get in the way of the powerful beatings he administered to his wife and children when he was on the sauce.

It wasn't just within the family that Stiles was known to be a drunken jerk. Most anyone who worked with him despised him. In a 2001 article in the *Columbia Chronicle*, promoter and banner artist Johnny Meah said that "Lobster Boy . . . was the most despicable person to work with . . . a chronic and abusive alcoholic . . . they couldn't find enough pallbearers for his funeral due to his horrible nature."

Eventually, Stiles's behavior got to be too much. Maria Teresa began taking solace in the arms of a sideshow dwarf, Harry Glen Newman, eventually conspiring to leave her husband and run away with the dwarf in the early 1970s. In 1973, Stiles, without reservation, granted her a divorce. She later married Newman, but that wasn't going to be the last she heard from Grady Stiles.

Stiles's disgusting nature surfaced in its most vile incarnation when he learned his oldest daughter, Donna, was going to marry someone he didn't particularly like. In 1978, Grady Stiles Jr. shot and killed Donna's betrothed the night before her wedding.

In court, he readily admitted to the crime, using his disability against the system. He knew that he couldn't be sentenced to prison because none were able to accommodate his condition properly. He broke his daughter's heart but never felt even a flicker of remorse; when he began to beat his family later in life, one of the threats he used on them came out of his perceived invincibility. "I killed before and got away with it, I can do it again," he would tell them. Grady Stiles was let off with fifteen years of probation.

After Maria Teresa left him, Grady married again. With his second wife, Barbara, Grady had a son, Grady Stiles III. He was born with ectrodactyly, and Grady was thrilled that his legacy would continue.

Unfortunately for Grady, lots of things continued, including his alcoholic and abusive nature. Barbara eventually divorced him, and Grady set his mind to cleaning up his act, which he did swimmingly at least for a while.

After a long time, Grady and Maria Teresa had finally learned to communicate and were back in touch with each other. Maria Teresa's marriage to the dwarf had not worked out and she found herself once again drawn to her ex-husband.

In 1988, Grady and Maria Teresa remarried. It was the biggest mistake either of them would ever make.

Like so many others in this generation of sideshow performers, the Stiles family settled down to start their brand new life together in Gibsonton, Florida. At least at first, everything seemed okay. Grady was sober and docile. But then, the lure of the booze became too strong for him and he started drinking again. It wasn't long before his violent antics resurfaced. As his daughter Cathy remembered of his behavior at her mother's trial: "[My father] was like Satan himself . . . very cruel, very cold-hearted, very sadistic."

Grady did horrible things to his family. Once, Grady the third remembered having to rescue his stepmother: "My father was on top of her, choking her," he recalled.

Grady's luck ran out when Maria reached her limit. She and her stepson, Harry Glen Newman, decided that Grady had to go, lest he finish off the family himself with his own rage.

On November 29, 1993, Stiles was gunned down by a hired assassin. A neighbor, Chris Wyant, a nineteen-year-old fellow performer (a human blockhead) was paid $1,500 in cash to take Grady out. Maria had left the family trailer and Grady was home alone, drinking heavily, smoking his Pall Mall cigarettes, and watching TV. It's possible he never knew what hit him when the three bullets cracked through his skull.

On December 3, 1993, Stiles was waked at the Hamilton Funeral Home in Riverview, Florida, and buried in the showmen's section of the Sunset Memory Gardens cemetery in Tampa, Florida. But the story certainly does not end here; for the widow and the children, this is the point where a new nightmare begins.

As many newspaper headlines were almost too gleeful to point out, the murder trial was a "circus." Maria was railroaded. She pleaded with the court, explaining, "My husband was going to kill my family. I believe that from the bottom of my heart. I'm sorry this happened, but my family is safe now. . . . At least I know they're alive, and I thank God for that."

It was to no avail. Wyant was convicted of second-degree murder and sentenced to twenty-seven years in the slammer. Harry Glen Newman was convicted of first-degree murder and took the brunt for being the one who orchestrated the whole clambake. He was sentenced to life in prison, without hope for parole for twenty-five years.

In what prosecutors deemed a "murder of convenience," Maria Teresa Stiles was convicted of conspiracy to commit murder and was sentenced to twelve years in prison in July 1994. (At the time of this writing, she should have already been granted her freedom, but if she was, newspapers haven't covered the story.)

With all that happened, the family feels no remorse for the death of Grady Stiles. "The night it happened and I found out my dad had been shot and was dead, I couldn't even cry," admitted Grady III. "I don't really regret my dad being dead because now we don't have to worry about the yelling, the beating and the threats."

Grady's daughter, Cathy, has a more bittersweet conclusion to draw. "Sometimes you are better off for the abuser to kill you," she says, "because you are not abused any more and you don't have to spend time behind bars."

NATURE OR NURTURE?

Melvin Burkhart

a.k.a. "The Anatomical Wonder"
a.k.a. "The Human Blockhead"
a.k.a. "The Two-Faced Man"
(1907–2001)

> If it doesn't kill you, you're a human blockhead,
> if it does you won't have anything to worry about,
> all your worries will be over.
>
> —Melvin Burkhart, on how one can know
> if he or she can pound a spike in his or her
> head, SideshowCentral.com

Beloved Melvin Burkhart was a friend to everyone, fellow performers and spectators alike. Years after his death, he continues to inspire and mentor a whole new generation of sideshow sensations, including Todd Robbins (see page 181). He was also the unofficial spokesperson for natural-born freaks everywhere. Said Burkhart, "No freak was a freak to me. They were my friends and we were all freaks together. I tried to be their shield against the world." And despite the efforts of those who believed they were doing the right thing, and put freak entertainers out of business, Melvin Burkhart did whatever he could to stay true to his word.

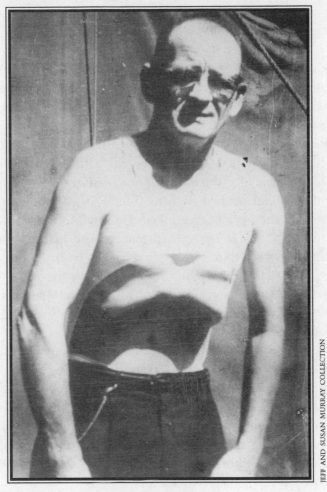

JEFF AND SUSAN MURRAY COLLECTION

Melvin Burkhart

Born Clarence Melvin Burkhart on February 6, 1907, in Atlanta, Burkhart grew up in Louisville, Kentucky. His parents may have considered him something of a "problem case," as he was always goofing off and trying to get people's attention. "I was a show-off, you know what I mean?" he admitted in an interview for Sideshow Central. "I couldn't sing, I couldn't dance, I couldn't tell funny stories. But I could catch attention by anatomical muscle control, which I didn't know I had at the time."

Melvin's family didn't understand or approve of his antics in the slightest; as Burkhart himself remembered, they thought he was a psycho, a troublemaker, and a hoodlum.

Burkhart thought differently. He left school before finishing the sixth grade. When he was fourteen, he got a job as a messenger boy for Western Union. Suffice to say, it wasn't his life's calling.

What Burkhart wanted to do more than anything was to join the circus. He especially loved the sideshow, but "naturally" normal, he really didn't see there being a place for him. Regardless, on his breaks, Melvin used to like hanging out behind the scenes.

One day, a door opened for him. There was a problem with one of the acts and the manager panicked. He saw Melvin standing there and he told him to get up onto the stage and just do something. "What am I supposed to do?" Melvin asked as he tripped up onto the stage and got a laugh. A lightbulb went off in his head. Burkhart pulled some more of his antics out of his proverbial hat. In addition to showing off what was to become his "anatomical wonder" act, he did bad magic tricks and made even worse jokes.

He was well received as an act, but his shtick really didn't catch on. So Burkhart turned his aspirations elsewhere. Still a teenager, Burkhart tried to become a professional boxer, but he was terrible. Burkhart remembered this detour for Sideshow Central. "They broke my nose and busted my lips and knocked out my teeth and I never won a one of them," he said. After no wins and six losses, all Melvin had to show for his efforts in the ring was a nose banged up so horribly he needed reconstructive surgery.

During the operation, for which he was wide awake, doctors removed a slew of shattered bone fragments (some say twelve, others say as high as twenty-four), giving Melvin an unusually large nasal passage. In time, after he healed, he learned that he could effortlessly pound a nail up through that passage—without causing any pain or damage to himself. How it occurred to him to try this and how he initially went through with it, however, is not known.

What is known is once Burkhart recovered, the Human Blockhead, and Burkhart's new life as a sideshow performer, was well on its way to becoming a reality.

As it was the first time he hit the sideshow stage, his act consisted of making corny jokes and performing silly magic tricks. It must be noted that there is one trick, however, that no one else has ever been able to figure out how to do. Impossible to describe; it involved dice. The secret of that one went to the grave with Melvin.

After he warmed up the audience with his magic tricks, he slipped into his "Anatomical Wonder" routine, which he coined his "Anatomical Blunder." Melvin discovered he could move the muscles of his face, each side independently of the other. "I could smile on one side and frown on the other and I could breathe through one lung at a time," he told *Shocked and Amazed*. Also, he was able to move his stomach in and out as if there were no bones in his torso. He says he got the idea when he was working out one day and saw a "before/after" poster and tried it out for himself. "I could pull my stomach way back in, which I don't do anymore. The doctor told me not to do that anymore."

In another variation, he could rotate his stomach muscles in a comical fashion, which he called "the cement mixer" or "the man without a stomach." Additionally, he could stretch his neck, as if it were made of saltwater taffy.

When the audience was all gaa-gaa over that, he'd offer up his pièce de résistance: With a hammer, he would pound a five-inch nail or spike right into his nose, without flinching, and he'd joke the whole way through.

Burkhart traveled with various circuses throughout the 1930s and 1940s, including the Conroy Brothers Circus, Ringling Bros. and Barnum & Bailey Circus, and James E. Strates Carnival, and also worked in "stationary" venues like Hubert's Museum in Times Square, New York, Ripley's Odditorium, and Coney Island.

Over the years, Burkhart added sword swallowing, snake wrestling, fire breathing, and other spectacular feats to his act, including knife throwing, a passion he continued to foster well into his eighties.

Suffice to say, Burkhart was a one-man ten-in-one. Truly, he had been known to perform nine or more acts out of the fourteen or fifteen that might be going on. He also served as a caller to draw in the crowds. He never missed a performance, which made him a very valuable asset to any show he happened to be traveling with; over the course of his career, it has been estimated that Burkhart traveled 900,000 miles to more than 100,000 sideshows.

When all that traveling got too hectic, Burkhart slowed down by limiting his work to Coney Island. In the interim, his friend Otis Jordan (see page 83) was kicked out of the show because a woman horrified by his "exploitation" demanded he be removed. Melvin went to the mat for the Frog Boy, as he passionately believed in the rights of anyone who wished to work as a sideshow act or an exhibit. "The sideshow gave incapable people an outlet to earn," he explained.

In 1989, Burkhart was forced to retire. More than anything else, his Anatomical Wonder act was wreaking havoc on his own anatomy; it was literally killing him. "I had a pulmonary embolism. Blood clots formed in my lungs," he explained in *Shocked and Amazed*. "You could die, but I was lucky."

Melvin retired to Gibsonton, Florida, the land of retired sideshow performers, with his wife, Joyce, and their three children. His first early marriage to a Cuban sword swallower known only as "Maria" failed. When he was forty-three years old, he met Joyce, who was working as a dancing girl in the James E. Strates Shows with him. She was twenty-three years younger than him, but neither Melvin nor Joyce really noticed or cared. They were married nearly fifty-two years—all reportedly happy ones.

Although retired, Burkhart could never resist pounding a spike in his nose from time to time, so he made sporadic appearances, darn close to literally up to his death. His last public performance was at the Sullivan Street Playhouse in New York City on October 8, 2001. He died November 8—just a month later, at the age of ninety-four.

Melvin Burkhart always said, "It takes something special to be a freak"; certainly, no one embodied that more than he did.

LEGENDARY IMPRESARIO

WARD HALL
(1930–)

He may be retired now, but in his career as a showman, which spanned more than fifty years, Ward Hall was a legend. While he never worked directly with Bettie Lou Williams (see page 106), Laloo (see page 97), and Schlitzie (see page 127), he's been exhibiting them for years (in wax).

Like Bobby Reynolds (see page 62), Hall made his fame as an accomplished "front-talker," who could make anyone come in to see anything. "Everything here is real," said Hall in 2003. "Some of it is real real, and some of it is real fake. But it's all real interesting."

At about age sixteen, Hall signed up with the circus. For several years he tried to go the traditional route, but it wasn't for him. In the 1950s, he moved over to sideshows, where he made a considerable living until retiring in late 2003.

In the 1960s, Hall took on a young partner, Chris Christ (don't know if this is his real name or made up). Christ was only sixteen at the time, but he made a considerable contribution to Hall's success.

Hall could see the changing perception of the "freak show" happening throughout his career. "Once the rock & rollers started calling themselves freaks in the Sixties, we used the phrase human oddities instead," he said in a 2003 article in *Rolling Stone*. "We didn't want to be associated with that crowd."

Their sideshow, Hall's World of Wonders, was based in Carny Central, Gibsonton, Florida. Several months of the year, however, it traveled throughout the country. In it, wax depictions of top sideshow acts of lore coexist with various oddities. Hall's only *live* performers numbered about three or four. There was a 700-plus-pound fat man, Harold Huge (Bruce Snowdon); a dwarf, Poobah (Norbert Terhurn) who's been in the sideshow business since the

1940s; a magician named Mystic Marlow (Stephen Baker); and a fire eater, Professor Chumley (John LeBrun), who is also a human blockhead and pincushion.

The changing climate of the world and its reception to the idea of the sideshow is what ultimately made the men decide it was time to throw in the towel. As Christ relates: "When I was nineteen years old, I was the youngest owner-operator in the business, and now I'm forty-eight and I'm still the youngest. So what's wrong with this picture?"

Hall, who discovered Otis Jordan (see page 83), has some hope left that perhaps the sideshow will come back in all its old glory. "I'm hoping the kids will find a way to bring the freak shows back," he said in the same *Rolling Stone* article mentioned earlier. For now, it remains to be seen.

Celesta Geyer
a.k.a. "Dolly Dimples"
(1901–?)

> I ate. From the time I got up until I went to bed.
> —Celesta Geyer

Celesta Geyer, more commonly known as Dolly Dimples, had no qualms about being plus-sized, which is clear from the above quote and the way she lived her life—for the most part. It was very much the contrary; Celesta absolutely relished her size and she made no excuses for it. It was not a glandular issue with her. She was very frank about why she was oversized: She ate. A lot.

On average, Celesta was known to consume at least 10,000 calories a day. For breakfast, she might have half a dozen or more eggs, *plus* a half pound of bacon, *plus* a loaf of buttered bread, *plus* two

AUTHOR'S COLLECTION

Dolly Dimples

quarts of whole milk. By midmorning, when the hunger pangs came a'haunting, she sated herself with about six or seven bananas. A typical dinner could consist of a roast chicken, maybe two, and tons of mashed potatoes. "Sometimes I would eat enough mashed potatoes to feed an entire family of ten," she said. For dessert, half a cake or pie would satisfy for a couple of hours at least. She would usually finish whatever she started for dessert as a pre-bedtime snack and had even been known to take boxes of crackers to bed with her and chew herself to sleep.

At one time, Celesta took enormous pleasure in her gluttonous gorging, but after a while, it would become a necessity rather than a luxury. If she did not have her requisite 10,000 calories a day, her body would revolt. She would have horrible nightmares and painful stomach cramps. It would be like she was starving to death, which, clearly, she was not.

As Dolly Dimples, Celesta was large and she was beautiful. With her bustline of seventy-two inches, upper arms of forty inches, and peak weight of 533 pounds, she was widely regarded to be the "It" girl of all fat ladies.

When Celesta was born in Ohio in 1901, she was a normal-sized baby. There was no obesity in her family—immediate or extended— but Celesta started getting large right away. She just ate and ate. It wasn't long before she couldn't fit in the wee confines of a school desk comfortably.

Eventually, Celesta graduated school but had a hard time getting and keeping a job in the "normal-sized-and-appetited" world. Unlike her good friend Ruth Pontico (see page 178), Celesta wasn't to the sideshow born. But she was a grown—and growing—woman who needed to support herself.

A few years after graduation, she got reacquainted with Frank Geyer, a childhood friend. At the time, she was dating voraciously and had many men interested in her. But something about Frank was different. The more she got to know him again, the more she couldn't envision her life without him. They married in 1925.

In 1927, she and Frank attended the circus, and a career opportunity finally presented itself. Celesta was spotted (really, at this point she was 400-plus pounds—how could she be missed?) by the circus management, who offered her a very sweet deal for doing very little at all. Frank quit his job and became her manager.

The Geyers traveled for years with the circus, through which Celesta made more than $300 per day. This is where they met and became lifelong friends with Ruth and Joe Pontico.

Like the Ponticos, Celesta and Frank spent the off-season in Florida. Here, with their incredible wealth, they built a home perfectly suited to Celesta's globulous proportions. In addition, among other weight-conscious amenities, the house had concrete floors and steel-framed furniture.

In the 1950s, Celesta fell into ill health. She began having horrible dizzy spells and chronic pain. When she sought medical attention, the doctor was very stern with her. His message was crystal clear: If she didn't lose weight, she was going to die.

Celesta realized that she liked being alive more than stuffing her face and more than being a chunky celebrity, so she gradually weaned herself down to a mere 800 calories per sitting. Eventually, she managed to whittle down to 150 pounds—she lost nearly 400 pounds!

When she retired from fat lady life, she didn't leave the carnival life too far behind. Reportedly, she became a fortune teller and called herself Madame Celeste.

She also published a weight-loss book, *Diet or Die: How I Lost 400 Pounds*, in 1968. Unfortunately for her, people were not as obsessed with weight loss then like they are now, and the book bombed. It's been out of print for years, though it would be interesting to see what Celesta thought of carbs and if cutting them was really the answer; the woman lost 400 pounds. If anyone would know, surely it would be her.

Jennifer Miller
a.k.a. "Zenobia, the Bearded Lady"
(c. 1961–)

> I am a woman with a beard . . . not
> "the bearded lady."
> —Jennifer Miller, as quoted in
> the *New York Times* in 1995

Jennifer Miller is a renegade. In the age of electrolysis and Brazilian waxes, when fashion magazines and popular culture at large have deemed that having any kind of body hair—whether on man or woman—is about as attractive as being covered in writhing insects, she embraces the way Nature has decided she should be, and proudly

LES STONE/CORBIS

Zenobia, the Bearded Lady

sports a long, thick, dark beard. Says Miller, "The world is full of women with beards. Or at least they have the potential to have a beard . . . instead of spending the time, and the money, on the waxing, and the shaving, and the electrolysis and the plucking."

Her humor and irreverence are as much a part of her as her facial hair. "We all know someone who plucks," she says. "Pluck, pluck, pluck, as if these women were chickens!"

In the tradition of all the sideshow greats, Jennifer makes a living, in part, by springing off how Nature, or in this instance, society, has made her different. And she takes it to the enth degree. In her own unique way, she has made great strides in reviving what was good about the sideshow, all the while with a conscience about where they went wrong. And sometimes she'll even do it in an evening gown, to show off *all* her natural qualities. "I'm a ringmaster and a woman with a beard," she has said in Circus Amok, a company she began several years ago that performs in public parks throughout New York City. "I'm also wearing a beautiful gown. I love the glamour and the paradoxical, feminine-masculine elements. I'm saying it's okay."

Miller is more than a "woman with a beard." She is a self-contained ten-in-one in and of herself. Not only does she have the "bearded lady" aspect of her act, she is also a juggler, a skill she taught herself in high school with a book; a clown; a performance artist; an escape artist; and an impresario in her own right. Moreover, she is a staunch feminist, who delivers her messages in between her "tricks." Of what she does, she says "It's a strong, feminist piece of theater. Ten times a day, I address in the strongest, most forthright terms feminist issues of appearance and dress. I use the platform of the sideshow to defreakify."

Jennifer was born and raised in a hyper-intellectual family, in Hartford, Connecticut. Coming from a heritage of college professors, including her father, a professor of physics, her mother, a professor of education, and her grandmother, Jennifer was always very interested in pursuing a career in education, but she never went to college. In a way, Nature toyed with fate, and while she educates, it's not in the classroom, but on the sidewalks and parks of New York City.

By the time Jennifer was about seventeen years old, dark hair began to sprout from her face. At first, it was popping up sporadically; by the time she was in her early twenties, a full beard had grown in, which gave her some time to deal with what was happening to her. "I was beginning to see my beard as a process, not a medical condition," she says. "As I get older, I get more and more committed to the beard. Its fibers are woven in deeply with who I am."

When Jennifer was just twenty years old, she lost her forty-eight-year-old mother to cancer. Jennifer had always been close to her, so it was extremely difficult to get through. Jennifer's grandmother was not exactly comfortable with the pelt on her granddaughter's chin, so she made Jennifer endure a few very painful sessions of electrolysis. Whether it was the excruciating torturous pain, the exorbitant cost, or the pure violation of having to remove something she felt a strong sense of identity in, Jennifer decided never to remove her facial hair again. With the exception of shaving a couple of times for, ironically, circus jobs, she never has.

In her twenties, Jennifer embraced feminism as well as came to terms with her own sexuality. In addition, she, now highly comfortable with her beard, adopted a very matter-of-fact attitude about it. When asked why she has a beard, she tells people "It grows there."

For several years, Jennifer performed at Coney Island and took a real interest in the history of the sideshow. Though offended by the aspect of "wild people," she sees and understands the validity of many earlier acts. In an article for the *Village Voice*, she said: "The sideshow is folkloric form. I have loved studying that and getting to know it in the craft sense, from the inside. But it has an awful history."

In addition to her sideshow work, she's also appeared on TV, on *The Jerry Springer Show*. Reportedly, she wanted to do the show because Percilla Bejano (see page 196) was going to be on that day, and Bejano was a performer whom she had always admired.

Today, Jennifer is director of Circus Amok, a company that performs in public parks throughout the city. As Jennifer explains, "My goal has always been to create a circus that brings together high camp, classic vaudeville, clowning, post-modern dance, and queer theatre." Circus Amok is all those things. For her efforts, she's won an OBIE, an off-Broadway version of the Tony, and a Bessie, which is a New York dance and performance award.

Ruth Smith Pontico

a.k.a. "Baby Ruth"

(1904–1941)

> Eating with Ruth and Joe [Pontico] was a jolly experience. We all enjoyed every minute of it. There were no feelings of restraint when I was eating with Ruth. She ate even more than I. She seriously confessed to me that she always packed away as much as she could hold and then more.
>
> —Celesta "Dolly Dimples" Geyer on "Baby Ruth"

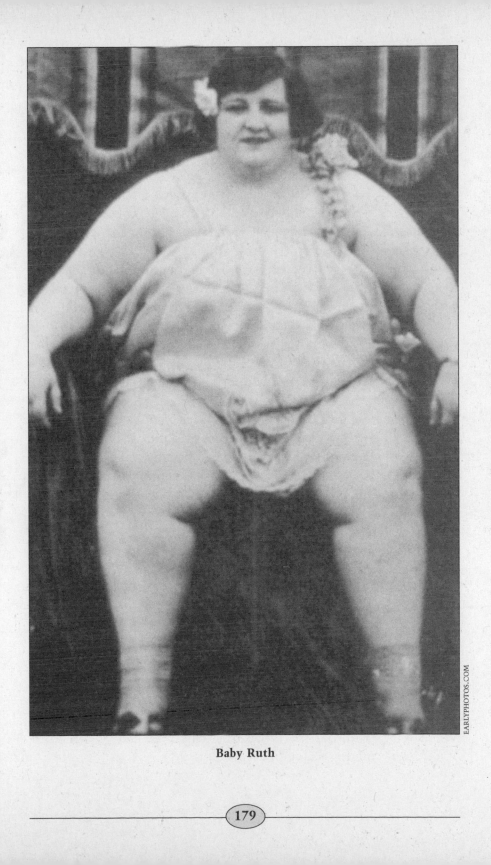

Baby Ruth

To have known Ruth Pontico was to love her. She was warm-spirited and generous, and an extremely gentle and kind-hearted person. What she was not, however, was particularly forthcoming.

The above quote by Ruth's good friend Celesta Geyer tells pretty specifically why Ruth was the size she was; Ruth, however, never owned up to it. Her mother was also a circus fat lady, and Ruth would try to make people believe that her weight was hereditary, a glandular issue, and not her fault. Anyone who had ever shared a meal with her, like Celesta, knew better.

Baby Ruth was born Ruth Smith in Kempton, Indiana. Not much is known about her childhood except that she was involved with the circus right from the beginning. This was the lifestyle her mother chose, and, for that and many other reasons, Ruth was always very happy working in the sideshow business. It suited her better than any other line of work she may have chosen.

At her size, she could not comfortably sit behind a desk all day nor could she do any kind of physical labor. And it certainly didn't hurt that she was really good at being a fat lady. In fact, if success for a circus fat lady can be measured in pounds, Ruth was a much more successful fat lady than her mother had been. At the peak of her weight, Ruth's mother weighed a mere 600 pounds, compared with Ruth's astonishing 815. By some reports, Ruth was desperate to get her weight up to 1,000 pounds and was frustrated that she just couldn't get there.

Ruth married but never had any children. She met her husband, Joe Pontico, when the circus played Madison Square Garden in New York City. For him, it was love at first sight. For her, well it wasn't as easy to spot a 130-pound balloon seller in the crowd, but once she got to know him, she fell deeply in love with him, too.

Joe loved her size—it's what drew him to her after all—and never encouraged her to lose weight. In fact, it was quite the opposite. Joe fully supported his wife's desire to be the biggest woman who ever lived, and he cooked rich, calorie-laden meals for her all the time. The food was so good, Ruth talked Joe into opening an Italian restaurant in Florida during the off-season, which he did. When Ruth retired, they moved to Florida permanently.

Now flush with free time, Ruth visited her sister in Muncie, Indiana, as often as she could. Unfortunately, she had a very bad experience on one of those visits. Her weight was so out of control that she actually fell right through the floor in her sister's living room. Because Ruth was so heavy, and no human was strong enough to rescue her from her imprisonment in the floorboards, she had to be pulled out with a crane. Her poor sister: The front of her house had to be completely demolished for the crane to reach Ruth. Needless to say, this was Ruth's last visit to Indiana.

Shortly after this incident, Ruth had to have surgery to remove a tumor on her leg. Sadly, Ruth passed away during the operation. Apparently, Ruth had ignored the instruction not to eat the morning before the procedure and got sick from the anesthesia while she was under. She choked on her own vomit as she could not flip herself over, or be flipped over by anyone in the operating room.

Ruth had a grand-style funeral, which proved she was much beloved. And it's a very good thing she had made so many friends in her lifetime; her coffin was so massive and heavy that it required an amazing sixteen pallbearers to lift and transport it.

Todd Robbins

a.k.a. "The Most Amazing Man in America"
(1958–)

> Todd Robbins is the kind of lunatic we need, not
> merely as entertainment, but in the way of a role
> model for our youth. A man who derives his income
> by hammering nails into his head with his own boot
> is vastly more important to the future of our society
> than the professional lampreys of Wall Street.
> —Alan Cabal, *New York Press*, 1997

Incredible showman. Fearless eater of glass. Bottomless sword swallower. Highly penetrable human blockhead. When it comes to doing what it takes to be a self-made sideshow sensation, you

COURTESY TODD ROBBINS

Todd Robbins

name it, and it's very likely that Todd Robbins does it—and if he doesn't already do it, chances are he'll give it a try. Says Robbins: "I'm willing to do it, like the guy who walks into a lion's cage or does a triple flip on the trapeze."

Robbins is a modern-day Melvin Burkhart and P. T. Barnum all wrapped up in one six-foot-four package. He hasn't missed the sideshow boat, he's heading up its exciting new voyage. As magician Penn Jillette says, "Todd is not just at the end of the sideshow business, he's after it."

Taking after his mentor, Melvin Burkhart, Robbins does all kinds of crazy things to his body, and in between stunts, he fills the breaks with the same brand of dry and at times corny humor that made Burkhart so incredibly lovable.

Born and raised in Southern California, Robbins didn't know right away that he would be swallowing lightbulbs for a living, although he knew he'd probably end up doing something unconventional. Robbins admits that he was "never attracted to mainstream kid culture. I was always intrigued with the quirkier side of things." Aside from his proclivity for the unusual, he essentially had a normal childhood.

One of the "quirky things" Robbins was interested in was magic. When he was twelve years old, he went to a carnival to take in the magic show, but he was sorely disappointed. As he remembers it, the magician was terrible. He didn't walk out on the show, however, and this was a very good thing because after the magician left the stage, the real show began.

The young Todd Robbins was treated to a spectacle, the likes of which he had never before seen. The performers began swallowing rods of fire and long, menacing swords. They were fearless—and they were highly entertaining. On that fateful day, Todd Robbins knew exactly what he was going to be when he grew up.

As an odd but lucky coincidence, a neighbor of Robbins's was a retired circus performer. The neighbor knew how to do all of the things Robbins wanted to learn and gave the eager boy his earliest lessons. "I learned it all," Robbins remembers. "With each skill I acquired, there came with it an understanding of the principles of physics and secrets of anatomy that make it all possible. It took hard work and persistence, to say nothing of burns and bleeding flesh."

After graduating high school, he attended the University of California in Long Beach, where he earned a degree in Theater Arts. Next, he attended the American Conservatory Theater in San Francisco, a training ground for serious actors. He didn't stay with it long. He knew there was nothing particularly "traditional" about the kind of performing he wanted to do.

Robbins moved to New York City in the mid-1980s. After a short while, he made his way to Coney Island, where he was a regular performer for many years. Most famous trick: he ate lightbulbs. When he worked more regularly at Coney Island, he admits that he could swallow hundreds per day. Now, he eats about fifty a week.

These days, Robbins makes only the rare performance at Coney Island. However, he remains heavily associated with the park. As the dean of the Coney Island Sideshow School, Robbins gives classes to train aspiring performers in the circus arts.

Todd started his off-Broadway show, *Carnival Knowledge*, in 2002, and it continues to draw crowds. He's done lots of TV, including the *Today* show. He loves every minute of his modern-day ten-in-one. As he says, "That's what really makes this all worthwhile is the look on people's faces—it makes the whole ordeal worth doing."

In *Carnival Knowledge*, he is both "ringmaster" and performer, and he dots his performances with quick and at times surprising quips about what he does.

For instance, of the human blockhead routine he performs, he says: "It feels so good after it stops hurting . . . it's a good way to get iron in your system." To help his body cope with the up-the-nose nail pounding, he uses saline spray. Of flame swallowing, he advises "Do not inhale the flame. Inhaling is very bad." To help his body deal with the fire swallowing, he ingests charcoal tablets. To offset the effect of swallowed glass in his system, he carefully washes the shards out with a cocktail of water, herbs, and fiber.

Robbins is proud to have played his part in bringing the sideshow back into the popular consciousness. He believes it's good for people. "When [the audience] are amazed they begin to wonder," he explains. "When they wonder they start to think, and this is good because there's very little thinking going on in the world today."

Tattooed Talents

Oh Lydia, oh Lydia, say, have you met Lydia?
Lydia The Tattooed Lady.
She has eyes that folks adore so,
and a torso even more so.

—"Lydia the Tattooed Lady" by Harold Arlen
and E. Y. Harburg, from *At the Circus* (1939)

When the first tattooed person was exhibited, the concept was so rare that people lined up around the block to see what a person absolutely covered in tattoos looked like. Around the end of the nineteenth century, tattooed talents made small fortunes displaying themselves—and the more tattoos, and more intricate the tattoos, the better.

By the turn of the twentieth century, tattooing had become more commonplace. The introduction of an electronic tattoo machine made body art accessible to anyone, quickly and painlessly. The novelty—the rarity—was gone.

Still, tattooed talents continued to make good livings; it just wasn't the windfall that it had once been, and therefore, less people were apt to decorate their body with colored ink. A tattooed lady, however, could always draw a significant number of gawkers.

Following are some of the most famous of the tattooed talents. (The Enigma and Katzen, two of the most famous tattooed performers today, will be covered in chapter 8, "Memorable Match-Ups.")

Betty Broadbent

The most famous of all the tattooed women who ever worked the sideshow, Betty Broadbent was the first person ever inducted into the Tattoo Hall of Fame. When she received this honor in 1981, she had already been retired from circus life for nearly fifteen years and was working as a tattoo artist in Good ol' Gibsonton, Florida. Upon hearing the news, she commented "Boy, do I miss the people and the travel." After all that time, she never got the sideshow out of her blood.

Betty received her first tattoo when she was fourteen years old. At the time, she was working as a nanny in Atlantic City. One day she was passing time strolling the boardwalk and met Jack Redcloud, a tattoo artist; he talked her into getting her first tattoo. It didn't take much coaxing. She loved the way the ink looked in her skin and was one of the first people ever to be tattooed by machine. By 1927, at just barely eighteen years old, Betty was nearly covered from head to toe. She would eventually accumulate 350 tattoos all over her body, but never on her face.

Betty's special gimmick was that most of her tattoos were illustrations of famous people of the time. She was certainly a sight to behold, and circus promoters did not miss her. She traveled with many outfits, including Ringling Bros. and Barnum & Bailey Circus, Cole Brothers, Sells-Floto, and Harry Carey's Wild West Show. For an astounding forty years, she traveled the globe, to lands as far away as Australia and New Zealand.

When she retired from sideshow life, she initially moved to San Francisco, where she worked as a tattoo artist. Years later, she made her final move to Gibsonton, and lived in the company of her fellow freaks until her death in 1983.

Captain Constentenus

With roughly 388 interconnected tattoos, Alexandrinos Constentenus, also known as Prince Constantine and George Constantine, was the most tattooed man of all time. He was also the first person ever to be tattooed all over as a way to make a living. According to a description of him in *Freaks, Geeks, & Strange Girls*, he was covered in "388 symmetrically arranged and closely interwoven images that covered his entire body, including his face, eyelids, ears, and penis." Reportedly, the illustrations were of nature motifs, with animals and various flora. In addition, he had writing between his fingers with supposedly provocative messages.

In his autobiographical pamphlet, caddish Constentenus spins several different yarns about how he got all the pictures on his body and how he survived to make it to the sideshow stage. To make a long story short, according to the pamphlet, after enduring several life trials and tortures he ended up as a prisoner in an Egyptian harem. There, he was pinned down for hours at a time while hundreds of pictures were forced onto his skin. He later admitted that he had hired Spanish and Italian tattoo artists to perform the arduous task.

How he came to be an exhibit in the American sideshow is also a mystery. Some accounts say the Great Farini (see page 118) found him and scooped him up. Others claim it was Barnum who first exhibited him. Accounts also vary as to whether he made his first appearance in 1870 or 1873.

Whatever the case, he was hugely successful, raking in an amazing $1,000 per week in the late 1800s. Considering the average American household income in 2001 was $53,100, roughly $1,021 per week, it's not a stretch to say that he was doing pretty well for himself.

No one knows what happened to Constentenus; however, his legacy was not lost. He inspired many other tattooed talents to ink themselves, including Irene Woodward, whom you'll read about later.

Nora Hildebrandt

The daughter of Martin Hildebrandt, who spent the Civil War decorating soldiers from the North and the South with tattoos, made her first appearance on the sideshow stage in 1882 at the Bunnells Museum in New York City, and is known as the first-ever tattooed woman.

Of course, it would be totally improper for Nora to admit she *wanted* to be tattooed, so she made up a ridiculous story that she and her father were captured by Sitting Bull, who commanded Martin to deface his daughter in such a hideous fashion.

Nora didn't enjoy her fame very long. As soon as Irene Woodward (see page 188) came on to the scene, there was just not going to be any competition.

The Great Omi

No one knows the real name of this sideshow groupie who, in the late 1920s, reportedly paid $3,000—though he boasted $10,000—to have his entire body covered with black and dark blue zebra stripes. The tattooing took about 500 sittings to complete.

Whether or not he ever made his investment back, the Great Omi did enjoy a decade-long or so career realizing his dream of being a freak in the sideshow, both with Ringling Bros. and Barnum & Bailey Circus and at Ripley's Odditorium.

Irene Woodward

Known to audiences as "La Belle," Irene Woodward was born in 1862. Reportedly, she begged her father, a tattoo artist, to cover her in color and images despite the pain it caused. She exhibited in 1882 as "The First and Only Tattooed Lady," which is only partially true. Nora Hildebrandt was the first, but Irene caused such a sensation that Nora quit when her rival appeared on the scene. So, yes, for a while, Irene was the only one. Irene was a sensation and made an incredible salary. She exhibited herself nearly till the end of her life at age fifty-three.

MEMORABLE MATCH-UPS

Anna Swan and Martin van Buren Bates

Anna Swan

a.k.a. "The Infant Giantess"
a.k.a. "The Nova Scotia Giantess"
a.k.a. "The Tallest Woman in the World"
(1846–1888)

Martin van Buren Bates

a.k.a. "The Kentucky Giant"
(1837–1919)

> Love is something eternal. . . .
> The aspect may change,
> But not the essence.
> —Vincent Van Gogh

Anna Swan and Martin van Buren Bates were literally made for one another. Known to the present day as the "World's Tallest Married Couple," they are also known as the only giant couple to ever have had a baby; in fact, they had two, although neither survived, as you will see later.

Anna Swan was born in the Mill Brook area of New Annan, Nova Scotia, Canada. On August 6, 1846, mother Anna Graham Swan, who herself was only about five feet, three inches tall, delivered, by natural means, an enormous baby girl. Unlike most of the giants featured in this book, Anna started out oversized. At her birth, she was eighteen pounds, whereby an average newborn at that time weighed between six and seven pounds.

There was no history of giantism in the family. At five feet, seven inches, Anna's father, Alexander Swan, was not that much taller than his petite wife. Miraculously, Anna's birth did not affect her tiny mother's ability to have more children. Anna was the third of thirteen children in that family. The remaining siblings were of normal height.

In terms of growing, Anna hit the ground, or the sky as the case may be, running. By the time she was three years old, she was already four feet, six inches tall and weighed ninety-four pounds. At age eight, Anna was her mother's size and could even wear her mother's clothes.

Unlike the family of Robert Wadlow (see page 33), Anna's parents were thrilled at the prospect of "showing off" their Canadian colossus, and they didn't wait long to do it. Alexander Swan took his daughter to Halifax in 1851, when she was just four years old. Even though Anna was not opposed to being an exhibition, she did crave some semblance of a normal life. When she was a child touring around with her father, she imagined that she would one day settle down with a husband and have lots of children.

By age fifteen, Anna figured out what she wanted to do with her life. She wanted to teach, so she enrolled in a teaching program. Unfortunately, this didn't work out for her. She had no trouble doing the work, but she could barely squeeze herself into the tiny desks in the classroom, or even into the classroom itself. And she hadn't finished growing yet.

Anna had to face facts: The more she grew, the more obvious it became that she was not destined to lead the "normal" life she had always dreamed of. But she was okay with that. She wasn't sure what life would bring, but she was ready for it.

By age sixteen, Anna was nearly full grown at seven feet, eleven inches. This was the year that Anna was spotted by a scout for P. T. Barnum. As soon as he saw her, he sent back word to Barnum, who was excited and determined to have Anna come to New York to exhibit at his American Museum.

Anna was tepid at best about the idea. Although her early experience as a human exhibit was not traumatic in any way, it wasn't what she saw for herself in life. And even though the scout made her a generous offer, she told him that she was not interested.

Over the course of the next couple of weeks, however, the opportunity kept popping into her head. It could not be denied that joining up with Barnum would mean making a great living. Besides, Anna had always been interested in seeing the world, but a woman could not very well travel around by herself in 1862. However, with an entourage it would be perfectly acceptable. All of Barnum's big acts traveled across the United States and throughout Europe. Now she would have her chance. And the best part about it was that it would be on Barnum's dime. And who knew . . . maybe somewhere in that big world full of possibilities, Anna might even find a proper mate. Anna headed to New York with her mother.

From the minute he laid eyes on her, Barnum adored his giantess. It was the same as it had been for him when he first met Tom Thumb (see page 13) and Lavinia Warren (see page 19). According to some accounts, Barnum did not treat all of his performers very well, but he went out of his way to take care of his favorites, a category into which Anna fit. It could be said that he downright spoiled her.

Just as the scout had promised Anna, it was all good. Barnum arranged for her to have a suite of rooms upstairs in the museum, where she could live and not have to worry about paying rent or feeding herself. Her education could continue, because Barnum had hired a private tutor for her—and she wouldn't have to trouble herself with Lilliputian lesson rooms.

Barnum also sprang for music lessons so that the young giantess could have an actual "act." Barnum, who had had plenty of fun dressing his miniature people, had a new challenge with Anna and he was certainly up to the task. He bought Anna the finest clothing, specially made for her by top designers from around the world. She had it all—and in addition, she was even going to get paid $23 a month in gold.

Anna spent the next several years touring Europe with Barnum and several other of his oddities. Eventually, the touring stopped and Anna gladly settled into life in the American Museum.

Unfortunately, the peace would be short-lived. On July 13, 1865, a fire broke out in the American Museum, burning it to the ground. Anna lost nearly everything—her clothes, her books, even most of the money she had earned with Barnum: about $1,200. Of course, there was also her life. Anna was upstairs at the time and unable to escape through the usual route because the stairs had essentially disintegrated in the flames. She had to be rescued from her smoldering rooms with a ladder.

Luckily for Anna, she had been sending money back home, so she wasn't flat broke. Still, there was no big fat insurance policy that covered the damages and Barnum could not keep his acts clothed, fed, and housed until he rebuilt. He couldn't afford to. Barnum sent Anna back to Canada with the promise that when he was able to rebuild, he would bring her back.

In about a year, Barnum's second museum was completed, and, true to his word, he sent for Anna. Tragically, that museum would also burn to the ground. On March 3, 1868, Barnum's career as a dime museum proprietor was over.

After the second fire, Anna started touring on her own in Nova Scotia, where she didn't have to pay royalties to Barnum. Anna was tired of losing money to Barnum by this point. Despite this, Anna did team back up with Barnum in 1869 and worked with Barnum for the contract's duration.

Anna Swan was finally on her own, but it would only be a matter of months before she met the next man in her life, fellow giant Captain Martin van Buren Bates.

Nine years before Anna Swan came into the world, Martin Bates was born in Letcher County, Kentucky. He was the last of twelve children born to John Wallis Bates and his second wife Sarah Waltrip Bates, neither of whom had been particularly tall.

As is the case with most giants (with the exception of Anna Swan), Martin was a normal-sized infant. That didn't last very long, however. Almost immediately, Martin began to sprout; by the time he was seven years old, he was six feet tall and weighed a whopping 300 pounds.

And he just kept growing. By the time Martin was twelve years old, he outgrew the family home, and his father had to reconfigure the house, widening doors and such, in order to accommodate Martin's mountainous proportions. He stopped growing at seven feet, eleven inches, and maintained a pretty constant weight of roughly 525 pounds.

Like Anna, Martin had aspirations to be a teacher. Unlike Anna, however, he realized this dream and happily taught for several years until the Civil War began. In 1861, when Martin was about twenty-five years old, he enlisted with the Confederate Army as a private in the Fifth Kentucky Infantry.

Martin's gargantuan size made him a formidable foe for the Northern forces. It didn't take long for word to spread about this soldier, who came to be known as "that Confederate giant who was as big as five men and fights like fifty." As a result of his might and his amazing performance, he made captain within a couple of years.

In 1863 Martin took leave and decided to visit his family. What he came home to was a ghoulish massacre; his entire family had been tortured and killed. The only one who survived was his nephew, Sam Wright.

With the urge for vengeance, Martin went after the Union barbarians. He knew he couldn't take on the whole army, but he could at least do away with the people who had so mercilessly tortured his brother. Angrily, Martin tracked down each member of the band that had killed his family, hanged them, and commanded their families to leave the bodies strung from the trees.

Shortly after, Martin was captured by the Union Army. He was put in a prisoner-of-war camp in Virginia, where he would sit out the rest of the war. Upon his release, he returned home and realized with deep sadness that there was nothing left for him in Kentucky. The war had taken everything from him.

Martin convinced his young nephew, Sam, to run away and join the circus with him, and he did. The two sole relations headed to Cincinnati and joined the Wiggind and Bennoitt Show. A few years later, they jumped over to the John Robinson Circus.

As could be expected, Martin was a very popular attraction. There was more than the sheer "gawk factor" alone, however. Reportedly, Martin was an extremely outgoing and charming man, who, despite his wartime antics, had made many more friends than enemies in his life. Many of these friends were quite influential people, such as U.S. presidents Garfield and McKinley, as well as Queen Victoria, who called on him to visit her in England quite regularly.

At the peak of his sideshow career, Bates was raking in about $400 per month. Considering that his nephew, Sam, made only $50 per month, Martin was making an outstanding living as an "attraction." But that wouldn't be the only perk of working in the business. Because of his particular line of work, he made the acquaintance of Nova Scotia Giantess Anna Hannon Swan, who would become the love of his life.

In 1871, Martin and Sam headed to England for one of their command performances for Queen Victoria. Fate intervened, putting Anna on the same vessel as Martin. Their paths had crossed a couple of years before, but then it was more of a warm spark than anything else. Now, the attraction was explosive.

Martin and Anna fell head-over-heels in love with one another. By the end of the ship's journey, they were engaged. The courtship was, ironically, quite short: They were married that year in London at St. Martin in the Fields Church, surrounded by friends, including fellow performers Millie-Christine McKoy.

Queen Victoria presented the couple with extravagant wedding presents: a giant gold watch for Martin and a diamond cluster ring and wedding gown for Anna. The world embraced the delightful giant couple as they toured around for their happy honeymoon.

After touring with the show for several years, and keeping a home base in London, Martin and Anna decided it was time to head home. They didn't retire from the business altogether; they simply slowed down. Martin and Anna built a house in Seville, Ohio, designed to accommodate their specific proportions. According to Martin's autobiography: "I purchased a farm. . . . It consisted of 130 acres of good land. I built a house upon it designed especially for our comfort. The ceilings have a height of fourteen feet, the doors are eight and one half feet in height. The furniture was all built to order."

What was not meant to be, however, was that they would expand their family. Anna became pregnant twice, and delivered two giant babies, but neither lived. The first, a daughter, was born in 1872. She was eighteen pounds and twenty-seven inches long. She died shortly after birth. Rumor has it that she was placed in a jar of formaldehyde and exhibited as a "pickled punk." (Pickled punks were bodies of infant oddities preserved in formaldahyde. Sometimes the babies were said to be real, but for the most part, they were wax dolls.) This, however, cannot be fully confirmed.

In 1879, the Bateses had another baby, this time a boy. He was nearly twenty-four pounds and well over two feet long. He lived about eleven hours. That would be the end of their trying for a family.

Anna and Martin traveled a little more in 1880 to escape their empty nest, but then retired. They would make sporadic appearances from time to time, but they were weary of touring.

Anna, who had been emotionally ailing, was also suffering from tuberculosis. After she lost the babies, she was never quite right again. On August 5, 1886, Anna died from heart failure.

Martin was devastated at the loss of his wife. However, he remarried in 1887 to minister's daughter Lavonne Weatherby. His second wife was just over five feet tall and weighed only about 135 pounds.

The Kentucky Giant died from inflammation of the kidneys in 1919, thirty-one years after Anna.

Percilla and Emmitt Bejano

Percilla Lauther Bejano

a.k.a "The Hairy Girl"
a.k.a. "The Monkey Girl"
(c. 1921–2001)

Emmitt Bejano

a.k.a. "The Alligator-Skinned Man"
(c. 1920–1995)

> If I did, I'd be down in the tip with the rest of you
> instead of standing here on the platform making a
> good living.
>
> —Percilla Bejano on why she never shaved

When Percilla Lauther and Emmitt Bejano married, they billed themselves as "The World's Strangest Married Couple." This was a common convention when freaks wed; half-girl Jeanie and giant Al Tomaini (see page 205) also adopted this title, as well as many others. And like Al and Jeanie, Percilla and Emmitt had both already made names for themselves in the sideshow circuit before they even met. The marriage was just another dimension to place on already-successful acts.

Percilla Bejano was literally born into circus life—okay, maybe more like *abandoned* into it. She was born in Puerto Rico to a couple who had moved there from Spain. Reportedly, at birth, Percilla was already covered in the dark hair that would define her. Her mother was mortified by what she considered an abomination of nature and not an infant at all. Her father was a little different. While he was shocked by the excessive hairiness of his daughter, he still loved her.

Percilla's father wanted his daughter to have the best life she possibly could, being afflicted in her special way, and he learned that a traveling circus might just be interested in a hairy little baby. So he

Percilla and Emmitt Bejano

brought his young daughter to the people who ran the show, Karl J. and "Babe" Lauther.

Percilla's father developed a friendship with the Lauthers and was working out the details of giving Percilla over to them when tragedy struck: In a random act of violence, Percilla's father was gunned down and killed. Percilla now, for all intents and purposes, was an orphan. (Only much later in her life would Percilla have any contact with her natural mother.) But that wouldn't last long.

Karl and Babe decided to legally adopt the child and raise her in the business. Percilla took to show life almost as soon as she could walk and talk, and by the time she was school aged, her career was in full swing.

As an added gimmick, the Lauthers picked up a chimpanzee for Percilla, who was now touted the "monkey-faced girl," to perform with. Josephine the chimp was with Percilla for many years. In raising her, Percilla remembered she "trained her to ride a bicycle and smoke. She smoked cigarettes" (James Taylor's Shocked and Amazed!).

Though it wasn't part of her act, Percilla learned to dance when she was about five years old. How did she learn? By watching the girls in the hootchy-kootchy show. All and all, Percilla was well taken care of by her guardians and very much enjoyed the carnival lifestyle.

In addition to all her face and body hair, Percilla had the simian characteristic of two sets of teeth. These would eventually get in the way, requiring costly surgery to correct.

When Percilla was in her teens, she met a frequent customer to the sideshow in Havana, Cuba—Senora Rosalia Obrea—who had a penchant for primates. Rosalia became especially fond of Percilla and wanted to adopt the seventeen-year-old girl. She promised the Lauthers she would put Percilla through college and look after all her needs, including the operation on her mouth that she so sorely required.

Many different versions of what happened next have been told, and even Percilla herself hadn't quite remembered everything when she was interviewed by Taylor shortly before her death. For one, she didn't remember thinking there was anything particularly sinister about the woman. "Years later," she told Taylor, "the *Enquirer* had that I was going to be mated to a gorilla by that woman." Percilla said she didn't believe that. Even though the woman and her menagerie had creeped her out, she suspected that the woman was just lonely and "all she wanted from me was for me to be her daughter."

That's not, reportedly, how Percilla felt at the time. In another version of the story, the Lauthers tried to talk Percilla into going with Senora Obrea. They loved their daughter and wanted only the best for her. Percilla loved them too, desperately, but it wasn't just her attachment to them that made her want to give up a life of riches and comfort to stay with her dustbowl-roaming parents. There was something about Senora Obrea that Percilla just could not trust, and she fought going with her.

Touring with the Lauthers' show at this time was a handsome, young, alligator-skinned man named Emmitt Bejano. He had, without letting on to anyone, become very sweet on Percilla. When he heard there was a possibility that she would be leaving the show, he did the only reasonable thing: He proposed marriage.

Emmitt Bejano was born in Punta Gorda, Florida, around 1920. From birth, Emmitt had suffered from a skin condition that caused his skin to be scaly like a reptile. There's no information available as to what happened to his mother; his natural father died when he was still a child and he was adopted. It was his adoptive father who took him out on the road and made an act of him.

When Emmitt joined Lauther's show in the 1930s, he was immediately smitten with Percilla. Karl didn't like him because he liked Percilla so much, so Emmitt quit the show, as Percilla reports, "before he got fired by Karl Lauther." Emmitt didn't quit Percilla, however. After he found out about the situation with Senora Obrea, he was not about to lose his precious monkey girl. Percilla and Emmitt eloped in April 1838, because Lauther was very possessive over Percilla and didn't want her to marry Emmitt or anyone else.

Shortly after they married, Percilla gave birth to a baby girl, Francine Lauther Bejano, in Washington, D.C., but the joy didn't last.

The baby contracted pneumonia and died within a couple of weeks. They never conceived another child, even though some accounts say that Percilla gave birth to two healthy, normal children. They did, however, adopt a son, whom they named Tony.

Percilla wasn't the only one who adored Emmitt. Apparently, he was loaded with charm and personality, and despite his scaly skin, incredibly handsome. Emmitt impressed people everywhere he went with his looks and easy wit. When asked once if he was a college man, he quipped that yes, he did go to college. He "went in one door and out the other."

By the 1950s, the couple had their own show. Billed as "The World's Strangest Married Couple," they toured the country with their own entourage and, to keep up the mystery, Percilla always wore veils when she went out in public.

In the 1970s, Percilla and Emmitt got tired of all the traveling and retired to Gibsonton, Florida. With no more reason to have it, Percilla began shaving her beard.

In 1995, Percilla's beloved Emmitt died and she never got over the loss. She admitted to missing him every day of her life after he was gone until she joined him in death on February 5, 2001.

The Enigma and Katzen

(both are alive in 2004 and in their thirties; no birth dates or real names available)

> I just wanted to do something bit by bit, piece by piece.
>
> —The Enigma

> The tattooing never stopped me in any way, because I know the route I want to go for. I never once had doubts about it. It's opened so many doors for me. Good things happen all the time.
>
> —Katzen

COURTESY HUMAN MARVELS

The Enigma and Katzen

Talk about your "World's Strangest Married Couple"—certainly there's no one out there who could ever compare to The Enigma and Katzen. With their vibrantly themed bodies, artificial add-ons, and their shared passion for peculiar performance, they are soul mates in every way and they are strange.

Besides being full-sized living, breathing canvases, The Enigma and Katzen also swallow swords and breathe fire. Katzen is also a contortionist. These days, however, the two are focused mostly on their music, with the old trappings of their act thrown in for effect.

Both The Enigma and Katzen grew up with relatively normal lives. The Enigma, who lived in Seattle, explains about his childhood: "I was spending most of my life in the backseat of a car going back and forth to private lessons, you know, casseroles in the evening."

The older The Enigma got, however, the more the suburban life was not going to be for him. As the years went on, he found himself more and more pulled toward the performance world. "In junior high I stumbled upon magic books and all of these miracle things that you could do such as sword swallowing and stuff," he remembered. "So I decided to bring that art form into the next generation."

So he did. For years, The Enigma worked as a street performer in Seattle, Washington. In 1991, The Enigma got involved with Jim Rose (see page 204). They hit it off, and soon The Enigma was working as "The Greatest Sword Swallower in the World." He stayed with Rose for a while, but really craved doing his own thing. All in all, he was with Rose about eight years, on and off.

Without Rose, The Enigma expanded his act to include eating slugs and lifting weights with his eyeballs. (For the squeamish, it must be explained that this was not actually done with his eyeballs themselves—well, not entirely. What he would do was tie strings to quarters and stick the quarters under his eyelids. He tied the other end of the strings to the weights.) At that time, The Enigma was calling himself "Slug," because that's what he ate.

That winter, The Enigma had a job pressing shirts at a local dry cleaner. Perhaps it was all the steam, perhaps the boredom of the mundane task, but it was there that he acquired the inspiration to tattoo himself like a giant blue jigsaw puzzle. Well, maybe it didn't come to him right away, but the seed definitely germinated there.

Unfortunately for the unstoppable Enigma, no one he approached about the tattooing would do it. Not until he met a sweet Georgia peach known today only as Katzen.

Katzen always knew she was going to be involved with tattooing in one way or another. Her inspiration came from when she was barely old enough to be in school. "I saw myself in dreams with markings on my body," she said. "It started really young—before I was five years old. I can't exactly place it."

Like The Enigma, Katzen was also a street performer before she got actively involved with tattoos. In her act, she was a contortionist, a fire eater, and a juggler. So it was the tattoos that brought them together.

When The Enigma and Katzen met in 1992, it wasn't a romantic thing. She agreed to start him out on his puzzle mission. It was a business relationship more than anything else.

On December 20, 1992, Katzen started to draw in the jigsaw piece outlines on The Enigma's body. She was the only person he'd let do the work at first—though he eventually opened up to others, otherwise it would probably never have gotten done. Today, The Enigma admits to having been "tattooed by over 180 artists around the world."

All that tattooing takes time—try six hours a day for a month. Over that time, The Enigma and Katzen grew closer, but not quite close enough yet. He traveled a lot so there wasn't time to really bond for them; however, Katzen worked on The Enigma'a tattoos whenever he was available. And once she finished his outlines, she started on her own.

As Katzen explains, "I think that tattooing is one of the ways people can get to self-knowledge. I think that there are several ways to get to spiritual knowledge by delving and internalizing, and pain and pleasure are definitely keys to it."

The Enigma says that he wants "to be a good ambassador for the world of tattooing and I try to keep a big bright smile on my face for everybody, whether they are tattooed or not. I feel that it is definitely a responsibility of mine to let everybody know that we tattooed people are cool."

Eventually, The Enigma and Katzen fell wickedly in love and married. In fact, they re-marry every year, and always in a different way. They have a daughter together named Caitlin, who as far as anyone knows, at this point in her life, is tattoo-free.

LEGENDARY IMPRESARIO

JIM ROSE

Jim Rose is not like any impresario in this book. More than anyone in the past ten years, he's brought the concept of "sideshow" to a whole new generation and given it a near-Gothic makeover.

Think Rob Zombie meets Barnum when trying to figure out what is all the excitement about the Jim Rose Circus. Rose has all the promotion skills of the master: He knows how to make people pay to see what they'd never admit wanting to see, and he does it with such a stomach-churning bent, you're sure that Zombie, especially if you've seen *House of a 1000 Corpses* (2003), has a hand in it. Suffice to say, the Jim Rose Circus is not your mother's sideshow. On his website, Jim Rose calls his show "a mind-bending thrill ride." That may just be an understatement.

The Jim Rose Circus made its first big splash at Lollapalooza in 1992. There, Jim and his company turned the MTV audience on to the world of the sideshow and won the attention of famous rock stars, who invited the Jim Rose Circus to tour with them, including Nine Inch Nails, Marilyn Manson, Korn, and Godsmack.

Since then, the Jim Rose Circus, which *Rolling Stone* touts an "absolute must-see act," has been terrifying and thrilling audiences everywhere. As Jim Rose says when he opens the show, "Not since Christians were fed to the lions has a show been this dangerous and entertaining!"

Rose has made appearances on *The X Files*, *The Simpsons*, and other shows. He has his own show on the Travel Channel. A taped Jim Rose Circus is available on DVD, and he even has a best-selling book, *Freak Like Me*, for which film rights have been sold. The movie is scheduled for release sometime in 2005.

These days, Jim Rose makes his home in Las Vegas. In addition to his other pursuits, he has been a spokesperson for Gordon's Gin as well as a public relations consultant for top firms looking to tap into a younger audience.

In addition to being tattooed like a giant jigsaw puzzle, The Enigma has horns surgically implanted in his head. They were originally silicon, but when he learned that natural coral will actually "grow" if it's put there in place of the silicon, he replaced them. In addition to her jungle-cat stripes, Katzen has "whiskers" sewn into her face.

Together, The Enigma and Katzen have appeared on several TV shows, and The Enigma has appeared on many more by himself, including *The X Files*. The Enigma and Katzen played a recent birthday party of Ozzy Osbourne's and are hard at work on several movie soundtracks.

Neither The Enigma nor Katzen feels any regret about all the tattooing, and neither believes they ever will. Katzen says that "A person who goes in for a lot of tattooing and especially facial tattooing has to have a very strong sense of self. . . . I can't walk outside without people asking me 'who are you?' You really have to know yourself, which I think you should anyway." The Enigma has a decidedly less philosophical bent on the whole thing. "About the tattoos and all of it, people ask what happens if we change our minds?" he says. "That would be like getting a sex change and then changing your mind."

Jeanie and Al Tomaini

Bea "Jeanie" Smith Tomaini

a.k.a. "The Half-Girl"
(1916-1999)

> You'd be surprised how many weird people you can find in an audience who think they're perfectly normal.
>
> —Jeanie Tomaini

Aurelio "Al" Tomaini

a.k.a. "The Italian Giant"

(1912–1962)

> Q: How does it feel to be a giant?
> A: It's a living, being like this, but it's a nuisance trying to be comfortable in a world made for smaller individuals.
>
> —From Al Tomaini's pamphlet,
> "Life Story of Al Tomaini, Giant Boy"

It's very fitting that Al and Jeanie Tomaini would be the performers to round out this collection of fascinating sideshow acts. The Tomainis, especially Jeanie, were like sideshow royalty, both when they were performing and even years after their deaths. It was Al and Jeanie who established Gibsonton, Florida, as a place for freaks to retire to, and who kept it thriving.

And while they may have been "The World's Strangest Married Couple" on the outside, on the inside, they were perfectly matched. The stuff of their marriage, the sheer force of their devotion to each other and their incredible compatibility, also continues to inspire.

Jeanie Tomaini was born Bea Smith on August 23, 1916. She weighed in at a robust six pounds, four ounces—robust considering that she had no legs. Bea was born with amniotic bands syndrome, which WebMD.com explains as "an abnormal condition of fetal development in which fibrous bands of tissue that originate from the amniotic sac encircle and constrict certain fetal areas, disrupting fetal growth."

It wasn't just Bea's legs that were affected. Her right arm was shorter than the left and had no elbow. In addition, she had only two fused fingers and a thumb on her right hand, while the fingers on her left hand were webbed.

Bea was the youngest child of Nellie Pearl Kunkel Smith and John Homer Smith. The latter made a living as a housepainter, and generally lost it in every bar from his job to home. John's alcoholism caused much distress to Bea's mother, who would take in laundry and do whatever she could to make ends meet, all the while raising a household of seven small children, including Bea. The excessive stress would eventually catch up to this woman in a most tragic way.

That Bea had no legs was not a problem to the ever-chipper infant, who was happy, active, and loving. In time, her parents began exhibiting their half-bodied marvel. At three years old, she could do cartwheels, handstands, and somersaults, much to the wonder and delight of the crowds.

Even though she was supporting her family at a very young age, there was no other choice. "No matter what you made back then, it was big money," she explained, "and when you had a whole flock of kids, like my mother did, big money sounded good." Jeanie later admitted that she never felt exploited by it. "I had no problem with it," she said. "I enjoyed it."

The first thing to know about the Blufton, Indiana, native is that she never felt sorry for herself and never accepted others' feeling sorry for her either. When she was an adult, she always did her own cooking and housework and raised her daughters without any outside help.

Eventually, John abandoned his family for another woman. It wasn't a financial problem because the family's prime breadwinner had become Bea. But it still put an enormous strain on Nellie, who loved her husband even more than herself. In time, Nellie just couldn't do it anymore. At forty-six years old, her "heart had burst" and she died. Bea was about fourteen years old.

The children went to live with their father and his new girl-friend, but it proved too much for father; he committed suicide after about a year of having them back. His girlfriend desperately wanted to keep the children, but she wasn't permitted to, so they were sent to an orphanage.

In two years, Bea was adopted by Lizzie Weeks, which proved to be a very bad thing. Weeks and her husband did not adopt Bea for love; they knew who she was, what her earning potential could be, and they couldn't wait to exploit her.

Lizzie Weeks never let Bea be seen in public because she felt if people could already see her, why would they pay for the privilege? She was also not permitted to have any friends. The Weeks promoted Bea as a "little genie" and eventually changed her name to "Jeanie."

It was a grueling life for Jeanie. Sometimes she would do as many as fifteen or twenty shows a day. Additionally, Lizzie played all kinds of head games with Jeanie to hold her back. Later in life, it's easy to see that Weeks didn't do any damage to Jeanie's spirit. And Jeanie also played her share of head games with the woman in retaliation.

Soon, Jeanie met a handsome giant named Al, and everything changed.

Aurelio Tomaini was born on February 25, 1912, into a large, off-the-boat Italian family in Long Branch, New Jersey. His parents, Don Santo Tomaini and Marie Bossone Tomaini, owned a grocery store.

Al was a giant baby—at birth he weighed more than fifteen pounds. By the time he was twelve years old, he was six feet tall.

Soon, Al's growth was out of control. By the time he was a teenager, his clothes and his shoes, which were a size 22, had to be custom made. By the time he was eighteen, he was eight feet tall. Soon, his knees and feet were giving him trouble because of his size, and medical intervention became necessary. Al was put on anti-growth hormones that finally kicked in when he was nineteen years old. He was already eight feet, four inches tall.

That summer, Al, who worked in a pool hall, went to the carnival with his brothers. As fate would have it, Al was at least a foot taller than the giant on exhibit, and the owner of the carnival talked Al into signing on with the show for the summer season.

Al was intrigued, and he figured that if it was just going to be for the summer, what would the harm be? He soon learned that there would be no harm, only good. Al made a killing that summer, so the next spring, he signed up with another show.

It was here that he met Jeanie.

Jeanie and Al had developed a strong friendship, and just past that, there was also a strong attraction; despite their incongruous sizes, they soon learned that they were soul mates.

The two wanted to get married, but because Jeanie was still only twenty, Lizzie Weeks had to sign her consent, which she would not do unless she could attend the wedding. The three eloped on September 28, 1936, and honeymooned in Niagara Falls. When they got back, Al promptly took Jeanie away from her old miserable life, and Jeanie never saw Lizzie Weeks again.

"The World's Strangest Married Couple" (he was eight feet, four inches tall; she was two feet, six inches tall) signed up with Ringling Brothers in 1937. They worked extremely hard and saved every penny they earned.

The one thing missing from their already full life, however, was children. Both Jeanie and Al desperately wanted them. There was a pregnancy, but sadly, it terminated in a still birth. A few years later, Al and Jeanie adopted one, and then two, daughters. Their first daughter, Judy Tomaini Rock, is the grandmother of Alex Morrow (see below).

One year, their friends Joe and Ruth Pontico (see page 178) invited them to vacation in Florida with them, and Al and Jeanie were hooked. During the 1940s, they vacationed in a trailer camp on the Alafia River and realized that here was where they wanted to retire.

In a few years, they bought land on the other side of the river and opened a restaurant and campsite called the Giant's Camp, a name suggested by their good friend, Frank Lentini (see page 60). The restaurant is still there, in what is now known as Gibsonton, Florida.

When they retired in 1949, they devoted their lives to the Giant's Camp. Jeanie did all the cooking for the restaurant and Al looked after everything else. Sometimes they would come out of retirement to make select appearances, but for all intents and purposes, their life was now in Gibsonton. Al was police and fire chief of the town until his death at age fifty in August 1962.

Jeanie lived many more years past her husband, and devoted her life to speaking out for freaks everywhere, besides keeping the restaurant running. She died on August 10, 1999.

Jeanie and Al may be gone, but their legacy lives on. The grandson of their daughter Judy is keeping himself in the family business. Alex Morrow, who goes by the name "Alex Zander, the Junior Torture King," is determined to keep alive the traditions of the sideshow. As David Kushner writes in his 2003 *Rolling Stone* article, "I Was a Teenage Freak," "[Morrow]'s on a mission to keep the freak flag waving high, fighting to carry the torch. And swallow it."

Melvin Burkhart (see page 166) taught Alex the tricks of the Anatomical Wonder, and other freaks have contributed to his "education."

Alex, who grew up among the freaks, is not only comfortable with the lifestyle he's chosen, he knows no other way. As he told Kushner, "None of this ever seemed weird to me."

AFTERWORD

As we have seen, in the present day, the sideshow is experiencing a renaissance. While long gone are the days that natural-born "freaks" will ever be exhibited, the legacy lives on with performers and impresarios like Todd Robbins, Jennifer Miller, Jim Rose and others, who continue to entertain and delight with some of the old methods.

But, aside from the sideshow you know, there's the sideshow you don't. Think about it and you'll begin to see that the sideshow renaissance has been in full swing for years—it's simply wearing a new costume. What's also different is that the modern curiosity connoisseur never has to leave the couch to enjoy it.

Consider the modern daytime talk show, and the guests who bare all the intimate details of their lives simply because they have been given the opportunity to do so—and the more shocking the stories, the more outrageous the confessions, the better the ratings.

Network executives are today's impresarios, showcasing modern oddities who may not have excess limbs or unusual dermatological conditions, but who are sources of great curiosity—of shock and amazement.

Reality TV is the bally of today. All it takes is the push of a button on any given night, and all of a sudden, right in your living room, you're treated to "a spectacle, the likes of which you have never seen." Is an episode of *Survivor* or *The Bachelor* not a ten-in-one in and of itself? All those different characters, all those odd and compulsively watchable situations and character dynamics. . . .

To my knowledge, there are no groups sprouting up to protect the rights of the privacy-conscious-deprived. There are no efforts being made to "save" people from essentially making asses of themselves. Why not?

Go ahead: try to tell yourself that these people are not being "exploited" for profit, that pockets are not being lined with the procecds of the shortcomings and "overcomings" of others. Realize that what is true now was, for the most part, true then: What it all comes down to is personal choice.

People have the right to choose for themselves whether or not they want to expose their defects and difficulties for fame and fortune, for fifteen minutes of glory. And each of us has the right to decide whether or not we'll watch.

BIBLIOGRAPHY

Periodicals and World Wide Web

Adams, Noah. "Profile: American Dime Museum Shows Curios and Artifacts, Real and Fabricated, in the Style of 19th-century Exhibitions." All Things Considered (NPR).

Adams, Rachel. "Caught Looking." A Cabinet of Curiosities. Common-place.org

Alward, Mary. "Anna Swan." Suite101.com. February 1, 2004.

"Anna Swan." The Nova Scotia Giantess Archive. The Lost Museum. Chnm.gmu.edu/lostmuseum

"Anna Swan: Chronicles." Collections.ic.gc.ca

"Banners from a Different World." Columbia Chronicle Online. March 5, 2001.

"Barnum and Darwin." Helicon.co.uk

"Barnum, Phineas Taylor." FactMonster.com

Batt, Elizabeth. "The Elephant Man." Suite101.com. November 12, 1999.

Beshaw, Brad. "Hollywood Deathwatch: Melvin Burkhart." Tabletnewspaper.com

"Betty Broadbent." The BME Encyclopedia Online.

"Betty Broadbent." The Human Canvas Online. Library. thinkquest.org

"The 'Blended Tocci Brothers.'" Zygote.swathmore.edu

Braden, Frank. "The 'Wonders' of a Circus Side-Show." *Illustrated World*. January 1922.

Brown, Craig. "A New-Look Elbow." *Daily Telegraph*. December 20, 2001.

Carr, C. "Circus Minimus: Miller Wows 'em in the Nabes!" *The Village Voice*. July 14, 1998.

Cavanaugh, Andrea. "'Greatest Showman in the World' Fillmore Man a Legend as Frontman for the Bizarre." *Los Angeles Daily News.* January 4, 2004.

Chadwick, Alex. "Interview: Ward Hall Discusses His Retirement from the Sideshow Business." NPR Special. November 18, 2003.

"Chang and Eng Bunker, The Siamese Twins." Phreeque.com

"Chang and Eng Bunker." Biography Resource Center Online. Gale Group, 2001.

"Chang and Eng Bunker." Who2.com

"Chang and Eng Musical to be Staged Here." *New Straits Times.* January 17, 2002.

"Chang and Eng Takes on KL, Business Times." *Business Times (Malaysia).* March 1, 2002.

"Chang and Eng, The Siamese Twins." Zygote.swathmore.edu

"Chang and Eng." *Dictionary of American Biography* Base Set. American Council of Learned Societies, 1928–1936. Reproduced in *Biography Resource Center.* Farmington Hills, Mich.: The Gale Group. 2004.

"Chang and Eng." The Barnum Museum website.

"Charles Sherwood 'General Tom Thumb' Stratton." Findagrave.com

"Charles Sherwood Stratton." *Dictionary of American Biography* Base Set. American Council of Learned Societies, 1928–1936. Reproduced in *Biography Resource Center.* Farmington Hills: Mich.: The Gale Group. 2004.

Chiles, Andy. "Organisers Defend 'Freak Show' Exhibition Pictures." Ic Croydon.co.uk

Cichester, Page. "A Hyphenated Life." BlueRidgeCounty.com © 2000, Leisure Publishing Co.

CircusAmok.org

"Conjoined Twins." Sideshow Ephemera Gallery, missioncreep.com

"Constantine." The BME Encyclopedia Online.

Cooper, Glenda. "Presenting the Very Human—HUMAN BLOCKHEAD; Every Night for 50 Years Melvin Burkhart Drove a Nail This Size Into His Head. Yet He Brought Compassion and Dignity to the Bizarre World of Freak Shows." *The Daily Mail.* December 20, 2001.

Crane, Ben. "Tom Thumb Trade Cards." Tradecards.com

Culme, John. "Chang, the Chinese Giant." FootlightNotes.com

DisabilityHistory.org

Dixon, Arthur. "The Giant of the Hills: Martin van Buren Bates." *Independent Herald*. August 5, 1993.

"Eng & Chang, the 'Original' Siamese Twins." The University of North Carolina at Chapel Hill website. February 12, 2004.

"Enigma and Katzen." Tattoos.com

"Exhuberant Proportions." *Dimensions Magazine*. November 1994.

FamousAmericans.net

"Fejee." Sideshow-art.com

"The Feejee Mermaid." Museum of Hoaxes Online.

Findagrave.com. May 3, 2004.

Ford, Rory. "Beating the drum for the disabled." *Evening News*, Edinburgh, Scotland. August 15, 2001.

"Freak Unique: A Potted History of Fairground Sideshows." TheGalloper.com

"Freaks Trivia." British Film Institute Online.

"General Tom Thumb!" Advertisement, *Brooklyn Eagle*, August 24, 1848. The Lost Museum Online. chnm.edu

"General Tom Thumb." Peopleplay.UK.

"The Gentle Giant." AshleighHotel.co.uk

"Giacomo and Giovanni Batista Tocci—The Blended Tocci Brothers."

Gilliams, Leslie F. "Side-Show Freaks As Seen By Science." *Illustrated World*. October 1922.

Given, Larry. "Commodore George Washington Nutt."

Glover, Shelda Baldwin. "Aunt Millie-Christine McKoy." Shelda's Corner Online.

"Grady Stiles, The Lobster Boy." John Watson Management, February 1997. Silverchair news archives, Chairpage.com

Graydon, Royce. "Overcoming the 'Ick Factor'; Russell's Conjoined-Twins Saga Hardly a 'Sideshow.'" *Star Tribune*. January 6, 2002.

"The Great Farini." The Municipality of Port Hope Online.

Green, Richard. "Robert Wadlow, the Alton Giant." StLouis. about.com

Hartzman, Marc. "Melvin Burkhart: The Original Human Blockhead '94 & Still Banging Away." Sideshow Central Online.

Highbeam.com

"The History of Nutts Pond." Manchester Urban Ponds Restoration Program Online.

HumanMarvels.com

IMDb.com

"Irene Woodward." The BME Encyclopedia Online.

James G. Mundie's Prodigies, Missoncreep.com

James, Mel. "Farini: Thrilling Millions (1838–1929)."

Jay, Ricky. "Sisters, United: Step Right Up!" *New York Times*. 1997.

Jim Rose Circus Online

"Johnny Eck—The Half Boy." Phreeeque.tripod.com

"JoJo the Dog-Faced Boy: Man of the Week April 2–9, 2004."
    Wasteoftechnology.com

Joseph Carey Merrick Tribute Website.

"Joseph Carey Merrick—the Elephant Man." Phreeque.com

"Joseph Merrick." Who2.com

"Joseph Merrick: Medical Curiosity." Wikipedia.com

"Just a Little Help from My Friend." Sideshow Central Online.

"Kids Testify for Mother." *Newsday*. July 22, 1994.

Klug, Foster. "Museum Honors America's Sideshow Past." *AP
    Worldstream*. December 13, 2002.

Kojima, Emi. "Happy and Healthy at 100." *The Roanoke Times*.
    December 27, 2001.

"Krao Farini: the 'Missing Link.'" Dinotruth.com

Kushner, David. "I Was a Teenage Freak." *Rolling Stone*. September 4,
    2003.

"Lady Olga." Sideshow Central Online.

Laker, Barbara. "Roots Run Deep: Woman Traces Family's Rich, Sad
    History." Knight Ridder/Tribune News Service. February 9, 2003.

Laker, Barbara. "Woman Discovers 'Eighth Wonder of the World' in
    Family Tree." Knight Ridder/Tribune News Service. February 9,
    2003.

"Laloo the Hindoo." Steven Bolin's Vintage Sideshow Photographs,
    SteveBolin.com

"Last Traveling Sideshow to Retire After This Season." *AP State
    News*. NEPA News Online. September 21, 2003.

Lewerenz, Dan. "Last Traveling Sideshow Folding Its Tent."
    AP Worldstream. October 19, 2003.

"A Linked Fate to the End." *New Straits Times*. May 1, 2002.

"Lobster Boy." Badtasteusa.com

Loftus, David. "Gibton." Documentaryfilms.com

Macy, Beth, and Jen McCaffery. "Eko and Iko: The Remarkable Life
    of Willie Muse." *The Roanoke Times*. 2001.

Manhattan, Nick. "The World's Only." Ratconference.com

"Martin van Buren Bates." The Bates Connection. Angelfire.com

Masserant, Melanie. "Banners from a Different World." Columbia Chronicle Online. March 5, 2001.

"The Masters Tocci." Sideshow Ephemera Gallery. missioncreep.com

McClellan, Bill. "Lifelong Talker Brings His Show, Collection to Town." *St. Louis Post-Dispatch*. November 26, 2000.

McElaney, Margaret. "The Human Circus Attraction." Lasalle.edu

Meah, Johnny. "The Frog Prince." The Czar of Bizarre Online.

"Mel's DIY Nose Job." *Scottish Daily Record*. July 17, 1997. Highbeam.com

"Melvin Burkhart—A Freak with a Nail Up His Nose." Goodbyemag.com

"Merman, Feegee Mermaid." RoadsideAmerica.com

Montgomery, David. "Strange Attraction; As Sideshows Vanish from the Midway, a Film Recalls Their Glory Days." *Washington Post*. October 24, 2003.

Mott, Wm. Michael. "Demonseed: Changelings, Halflings, and Human Monsters." Metareligion Online.

The Museum of Disability History Online.

"Myrtle Corbin at the Moulin Rouge." Sideshow Ephemera Gallery. missioncreep.com

National Portrait Gallery, Smithsonian Institution Online.

Ng, Julie. "Freaks: Come One, Come All, Last Chance to See . . ." the11thhour.com. 2000.

Nickell, Joe. "Sideshow! Carnival Oddities and Illusions Provide Lessons for Skeptics." Committee for the Scientific Investigation for Claims of the Paranormal Online. December 1999.

Niedershuh, Karl J. "The Doll Dimples Diet." DimensionsMagazine. com. 1997.

"Nora Hildebrant." The BME Encyclopedia Online.

O'Brien, Tim. "Four Charged in Stiles Murder. (Grady Stiles) *Amusement Business*. December 14, 1992.

"Obituary of Melvin Burkhart; Fairground Sideshow Performer." *Daily Telegraph*. December 19, 2001.

"The Original and Celebrated Gen. Tom Thumb, The World-Renowned Man in Miniature." Advertisement, 1860. The Lost Museum Online. chnm.gmu.edu

"Phineas Taylor Barnum." Barnum Museum Online. Phreeque.com

"Phrenology of Tom Thumb." *Littell's Living Age.* October 31, 1846.

Price, Slim. "Frank Lentini." Sideshow Central Online.

Quayle, Steve. "Giants in Asia." SteveQuayle.com

RipleySF.com

"Robert LeRoy Ripley." Who2.com

"Robert Pershing Wadlow." Findagrave.com

"Robert Pershing Wadlow—Alton's Gentle Giant." Alton Museum of History and Art. Altonweb.com

"Robert Wadlow, Tall Man." Who2.com

"Robert Wadlow, World's Tallest Man." HazardKentucky.com

"Robert Wadlow, World's Tallest Man." RoadsideAmerica.com

Rock, Judy Tomaini. "Jeanie Tomaini." SideshowCentral.com

Rodell, Chris. "In Odd We Trust." ChrisRodell.com

"Samuel Gumpertz." PBS.org

Saunders, W.B. "Anomolies and Curiosities of Medicine." Zoraskingdom.freeserve.co.uk

Sceurman, Mark. "In Search of Zip the What Is It?" WeirdNJ.com

"Schlitzie the Pinhead." SideshowCentral.com

Schnur, Susan. "Transgressive Hair: The Last Frontier." *Lilith.* March 31, 1995.

Sharp, Deborah. "'Lobster Boy' Trial Becomes a Sideshow Itself." *USA Today.* July 19, 1994.

"The Siamese Twins Eng and Chang Bunker." Wilkesboro.com

Sideshow-freaks.com

Siegel, Fred. "On the Ten-in-One." The Drexel Online Journal. 2004.

Smith, Dinitia. "Step Right Up! See the Bearded Person!" *New York Times.* June 9, 1995.

Snigurowicz, Diana. "Sex, Simmians, and Spectacle in Nineteenth-Century France; Or, How to Tell a 'Man' from a Monkey." *Canadian Journal of History.* April 1, 1999.

Stanton, Jeffrey. "Coney Island—Freaks."

Strausbaugh, John. "Big Men and Hairy Ladies." News & Columns. *Shocked and Amazed! #6.* New York Press Online.

Swiss, Jamy Ian. "People & Places: Melvin Burkhart." Jamyianswiss.com

Taib, Shuib. "'Chang & Eng' Success Story." *New Straits Times.* February 5, 2002.

"Tattoo You." Dallas Observer Online. October 30, 2003.

Taylor, Ian. "Krao Farini: The Missing Link, National Geographic and the Stone Age Swindle?" FreeRepublic.com. December 1986.

"They Didn't Ask to be Born: Ward Hall Gives You the Straight Skinny on Punk Shows." Freakophile.com

"Thumb & Nutt Perform in Keene." Historical Society of Cheshire County Online.

Thumb, Tom. "Tom Thumb on Kisses." *Littell's Living Age*. January 2, 1847.

"The Tocci Brothers." Sideshowart.com

"The Tocci Twins." Etext.lib.Virginia.edu

"Tom Thumb (Charles Sherwood Stratton)." Barnum Museum Online.

"Tom Thumb." Encyclopedia.com

"Tom Thumb." Infoplease.com

"The Tom Thumb Archive." The Lost Museum Online. chnm.edu

Toulmin, Vanessa. "Freak Shows." Science Museum Online.

Treacy, Jeani. "The Enigma and Katzen Perform at the Bros. Grim Sideshow at Funtime Pier in New Jersey." Prick Magazine Online.

Twinstuff.com

Vance, Daniel J. "Disabilities." DanielJVance.com

Velasquez, Pedro. "Memoir of Eventful Expedition in Central America; Resulting in the Discovery of the Idolatrous City of Iximaya, In an Unexpected Explored Region; And the Possession of Two Remarkable Aztec Children." 1855. Bridegport Public Library, Historical Collections.

"Visit to Gibsonton—Home for Retired Sideshow Freaks." All Things Considered (NPR). July 2, 1994. Highbeam.com

Wecker, Danny. "Twins Were Joined in Life and Death." *The Cincinnati Post*. November 20, 1997.

"'What Is It?' Advertisement." *New York Herald*. March 19, 1860.

"'What Is It?' Advertisement." *New York Tribune*. March 1, 1860.

"Wife Claims Brutality in 'Lobster Boy' Slay." *Newsday*. July 13, 1994.

"Wife Convicted for Slaying Spouse." The Associated Press. August 30, 1994.

"William Henry Johnson—'Zip—the What Is It?'" Hollywoodstudios.org.

"Wilson's Pick: Baby Ruth." DimensionsMagazine.com. November 1996.

Wolf, Buck. "Florida Recount Sideshow: Clowns and Carnies Say, 'Don't Call This Election Fiasco a Circus!'" ABCnews.com November 18, 2000.

"World's Tallest Man Statue, Alton, Illinois." GreatRiverRoad.com

"Zip Grins in Death, Mask Off at Last." *New York World*. April 29, 1926.

"Zip, the 'What Is It?' Plays Host to All the Other Circus Freaks." *New York World*. April 6, 1914.

Books

Adams, Rachel. *Sideshow U.S.A.: Freaks and the American Cultural Imagination*. Chicago: The University of Chicago Press. 2001.

Bogdan, Robert. *Freak Show: Presenting Human Oddities for Amusement and Profit*. Chicago: University of Chicago Press. 1988.

Bondeson, Jan. *A Cabinet of Medical Curiosities*. Ithaca, N.Y.: Cornell University Press. 1997.

———. *The Feejee Mermaid and Other Essays in Natural and Unnatural History*. Ithaca, N.Y.: Cornell University Press. 1999.

———. *The Two-Headed Boy and Other Medical Marvels*. Ithaca, N.Y.: Cornell University Press. 2000.

Bone, Howard. *Sideshow: My Life with Geeks, Freaks & Vagabonds in the Carny Trade*. Northville, Mich.: Sun Dog Press. 2001.

Dunn, Katherine. *Geek Love*. New York: Warner Books. 1983.

Howell, Michael, and Peter Ford. *The True History of the Elephant Man: The Definitive Account of the Tragic and Extraordinary Life of Joseph Carey Merrick*. London: Allison & Bushby Limited. 1980.

Mannix, Daniel P. *Freaks: We Who Are Not as Others*. New York: Pocket Books. 1976.

Martell, Joanne. *Millie-Christine: Fearfully and Wonderfully Made*. Winston-Salem, N.C.: John S. Blair, Publisher. 2000.

Mitchell, Michael, ed. *Monsters: Human Freaks in America's Guilded Age. (The Photographs of Chas. Eisenmann.)* Toronto. 2002.

Monestier, Martin. *Human Oddities: A Book of Nature's Divine Abnormalities*. New York: Citadel Press. 1987.

Sloan, Mark. *Wild, Weird, and Wonderful. The American Circus 1901–1927. (As seen by F.W. Glasier, Photographer.)* New York: The Quantuck Lane Press. 2003.

Slouka, Mark. *God's Fool.* New York: Knopf. 2002.

Stencil, A. W. *Seeing Is Believing: America's Sideshows.* Toronto: ECS Press. 2002.

Strauss, Darin. *Chang and Eng.* New York: Dutton. 2000.

Taylor, James, and Kathleen Kotcher. *James Taylor's Shocked and Amazed! On & Off the Midway.* Guilford, Conn.: The Lyons Press. 2002.

Thompson, Rosemary Garland. *Freakery: Cultural Spectacles of the Extraordinary Body.* New York: New York University Press. 1996.

———. *Extraordinary Bodies: Figuring American Physical Disability in American Culture and Literature.* New York: Columbia University Press. 1997.